WILLIAMS-SONOMA
COLLECTION

RAVIOLI & LASAGNE

WITH OTHER BAKED & FILLED PASTAS

WILLIAMS-SONOMA
COLLECTION

RAVIOLI & LASAGNE

WITH OTHER BAKED & FILLED PASTAS

GENERAL EDITOR
CHUCK WILLIAMS

RECIPES BY
MICHELE ANNA JORDAN

PHOTOGRAPHY BY
JOYCE OUDKERK POOL

TIME
LIFE
BOOKS

Time-Life Books is a division of
Time-Life Incorporated

President and CEO: John Fahey, Jr.

TIME-LIFE BOOKS

President, Time-Life Books: John D. Hall
Vice President and Publisher: Terry Newell
Director of New Product Development: Regina Hall
Director of Financial Operations: J. Brian Birky
Editorial Director: Donia Ann Steele

All recipes include customary U.S. and metric measurements.
Metric conversions are based on a standard developed for this
book and have been rounded off. Actual weights may vary.
Unless otherwise stated, the recipes were designed for medium-
sized fruits and vegetables.

*Cover: Spinach Ravioli with Summer Tomato Sauce (recipe on
page 45) brings fresh produce together in an exciting combination.*

WILLIAMS-SONOMA
Founder: Chuck Williams

WELDON OWEN INC.
President: John Owen
Vice President and Publisher: Wendely Harvey
Managing Editor: Jill Fox
Recipe Analysis: Hill Nutrition Associates Inc.
 Lynne S. Hill, MS, RD; William A. Hill, MS, RD
Copy Editor: Carolyn Miller
Editorial Assistants: Stephani Grant, Marguerite Ozburn
Art Director: John Bull
Designer: Patty Hill
Production Director: Stephanie Sherman
Production Editor: Janique Gascoigne
Co-Editions Director: Derek Barton
Co-Editions Production Manager: Tarji Mickelson
Food Stylist: Susan Massey
Food Stylist Assistants: Andrea Lucich, Geri Lesko,
 Vicki Roberts-Russell
Prop Stylist: Carol Hacker
Photographer's Assistant: Myriam Varela
Hand Model: Tracey Hughes
Indexer: ALTA Indexing Service
Proofreaders: Desne Border, Ken DellaPenta
Illustrator: Nicole Kaufman
Writer's Photographer: David Licht
Props Courtesy: Biordi, Bryan's Meats, Cal-Mart,
 Pottery Barn, Williams-Sonoma
Special Thanks: Mick Bagnato, John Boland,
 James Carroll, Betty Ellsworth, Peggy Fallon,
 Leisel Hofman, Jane Lawrence, Ginny Stanford,
 Michel Stong, Jon Stong, Lesa Tanner

A Weldon Owen Production

First printing in 1996
10 9 8 7 6 5 4 3 2 1

Library of Congress
Cataloging-in-Publication Data:

Jordan, Michele Anna.
 Ravioli and lasagne / general editor, Chuck Williams ;
 recipes, Michele Anna Jordan ; photography by
 Joyce Oudkerk Pool.
 p. cm. — (Williams-Sonoma pasta collection)
 Includes index.
 ISBN 0-7835-0312-1
 1. Cookery (Pasta) 2. Stuffed foods (Cookery)
 I. Williams, Chuck. II. Title. III. Series.
 TX809.M17J673 1996
 641.8'22—dc20   95-31193
                        CIP

The Williams-Sonoma Collection
conceived and produced by Weldon Owen Inc.
814 Montgomery Street, San Francisco, CA 94133

In collaboration with Williams-Sonoma
3250 Van Ness Avenue, San Francisco, CA 94109

Production by Mandarin Offset, Hong Kong
Printed in China

CONTENTS

Pasta Basics 6

The Pleasures of Baked and Filled Pastas 8 Making Fresh Pasta 10

Using Dried Pasta 16 Cooking Perfect Pasta 18

Ravioli 20

Lasagne and Baked Pastas 46

Filled Pastas 82

Basic Terms and Techniques 116

Basic Recipes 123

Index 128

Pasta Basics

THE PLEASURES OF BAKED AND FILLED PASTAS

From plump ravioli bursting with a moist and flavorful filling to generous tubes of cannelloni stuffed with cheese and blanketed with sauce, from tender crespelle wrapped around seasonal vegetables to a robust lasagne served in ample squares, the pleasures of pasta abound. Widely varied as these dishes are, they share a common attribute. They elevate pasta—both fresh and dried—to an extraordinary eating experience. The ravioli, lasagne and other baked and filled pasta recipes that follow provide that abundantly.

RAVIOLI

Filled pastas present a delicious assortment of pasta packages including both square and round ravioli (recipes begin on page 20) plus tortellini and the Italian pancakes called crespelle as well as various dried pasta tubes and shapes stuffed with wondrous fillings (recipes begin on page 84). Ravioli, tortellini, crespelle and cannelloni are best made from fresh pasta you've prepared at home yourself (see pages 10–13). If pressed for time, purchase sheets of fresh pasta. Wonton wrappers, which are made from a dough similar to fresh pasta, may be substituted in many ravioli recipes. It is essential to make sure that filled pastas are tightly sealed along their edges before you cook them. Even a tiny opening will let some of the cooking water seep in and dilute the filling. Carefully follow the sealing instructions given on pages 14–15.

Ravioli can be made ahead and refrigerated in a tightly covered container for up to 2 days or frozen for several months. To do so, arrange them on a baking sheet, not touching each other, and freeze until hard. Then transfer them to a freezer bag. Do not defrost; cook them from the frozen state.

LASAGNE

Baked pastas comprise a variety of hearty dishes including lasagne, soufflés, flans, pasta cooked in parchment and soups topped with crusts and heated in the oven (recipes begin on page 46). These dishes make beautiful presentations and can be prepared hours in advance, refrigerated, then baked at the last minute, making them ideal choices for entertaining. They can be frozen for several months as well. In both cases, allow the dish to cool completely after forming and cover with aluminum foil. Bring to room temperature before baking.

NUTRITIONAL ANALYSIS

Each recipe in this book has been evaluated by a registered dietitian. The resulting analysis lists the nutrient breakdown per serving. Use these numbers to plan nutritionally balanced meals. All ingredients listed with each recipe have been included in the analysis. Exceptions are items inserted "to taste" and those listed as "optional."

When seasoning with salt, bear in mind that each teaspoon of regular salt contains 2,200 mg of sodium. The addition of black or white pepper does not alter nutrient values. Substituted ingredients, recipe variations and accompaniments suggested in the recipe introductions or shown in the photographs have not been included in the analysis.

NUTRITIONAL TERMS

CALORIES (KILOJOULES)
Calories provide a measure of the energy provided by any given food. A calorie equals the heat energy necessary to raise the temperature of 1 kg of water by 1°Celsius. One calorie is equal to 4.2 kilojoules—a term used instead of calories in some countries.

PROTEIN
One of the basic life-giving nutrients, protein helps build and repair body tissues and performs other essential functions. One gram of protein contains 4 calories. A healthy diet derives about 15 percent of daily calories from protein.

CARBOHYDRATES
Classed as either simple (sugars) or complex (starches), carbohydrates are the main source of dietary energy. One gram contains 4 calories. A healthy diet derives about 55 percent of daily calories from carbohydrates, with not more than 10 percent coming from sugars.

TOTAL FAT
This number measures the grams of fat per serving, with 1 gram of fat equivalent to 9 calories, more than twice the calories present in a gram of protein or carbohydrate. Experts recommend that total fat intake be limited to a maximum of 30 percent of total daily calories.

SATURATED FAT
Derived from animal products and some tropical oils, saturated fat has been found to raise blood cholesterol and should be limited to no more than one-third of total daily fat calories.

CHOLESTEROL
Cholesterol is a fatty substance present in foods of animal origin. Experts suggest a daily intake of no more than 300 mg. Plant foods contain no cholesterol.

SODIUM
Derived from salt and naturally present in many foods, sodium helps maintain a proper balance of body fluids. Excess intake can lead to high blood pressure, or hypertension, in sodium-sensitive people. Those not sensitive should limit daily intake to about 2,200 mg.

FIBER
Dietary fiber aids elimination and may help prevent heart disease, intestinal disease and some forms of cancer. A healthy diet should include 20–35 grams of fiber daily.

Making FRESH PASTA

Fresh pasta can be made at home using a food processor and a reasonably priced, manual pasta machine in about 10 minutes. The machine method is described in the instructions at right and shown in the step-by-step photographs on page 12. Pasta can be made by hand as well (see page 13). Use the Egg Pasta recipes and the instructions at right as the basis for making all fresh pasta. To flavor the pasta, change the ingredients as noted for each variation.

PASTA INGREDIENTS

Semolina flour is made from durum, the hardest wheat grown, and is not bleached; for pasta making, be sure to purchase the finely ground variety—often called pasta flour—not coarse-ground semolina. The flour is high in gluten, which provides the elasticity necessary for kneading, cutting and shaping fresh pasta. All-purpose (plain) flour is a blend of wheat flours and has a finer feel than semolina flour. While fresh pasta can be made with only all-purpose flour, the addition of semolina flour gives the finished pasta a firmer texture.

Either common table salt or coarser kosher salt can be used when making fresh pasta. Use large Grade A eggs, which should be at room temperature to blend with the flour more easily.

Depending on the temperature and humidity of the kitchen, you may need to add some water when combining the ingredients so that the dough forms a ball properly. If the ball is too sticky, add more flour.

ONE-POUND EGG PASTA

Depending on the sauce, 1 lb (500 g) of pasta serves 4–6 as a main course or 6–8 as a first course or side dish.

1⅓ cups (7 oz/220g) semolina flour

⅔ cup (4 oz/125 g) unbleached all-purpose (plain) flour plus additional for dusting

¼ teaspoon salt

2 eggs at room temperature

1½ tablespoons water

BLACK PEPPER PASTA Add 2 teaspoons freshly ground pepper.

BEET PASTA Replace the water with ⅓ cup (3 fl oz/80 ml) cooked beet purée.

LEMON PASTA Replace the water with 1½ tablespoons fresh lemon juice and add 1 tablespoon grated lemon zest.

SAFFRON PASTA Soak ⅛ teaspoon saffron threads in the 1½ tablespoons water for 30 minutes before using.

SPINACH PASTA Replace the water with 1 cup (1 oz/30 g) loosely packed spinach leaves, steamed, squeezed dry and chopped.

TOMATO PASTA Replace the water with 2 tablespoons concentrated tomato paste.

Each recipe makes 1 lb (500 g)

POUND-AND-A-HALF EGG PASTA

Depending on the sauce, 1½ lb (750 g) of pasta serves 6–8 as a main course or 8–10 as a first course or side dish.

2 cups (10 oz/315 g) semolina flour
1 cup (5 oz/155 g) unbleached all-purpose (plain) flour plus additional for dusting
½ teaspoon salt
3 eggs at room temperature
3 tablespoons water

MAKING PASTA BY MACHINE

1. In the work bowl of a food processor with the metal blade, combine all the ingredients from the recipes. Pulse several times to incorporate.

2. Using a rubber spatula, scrape down the sides of the work bowl. Pulse a few more times for a few seconds each time, until the dough forms a soft ball, but is not sticky. Add more water or flour, if necessary.

3. To knead the dough, remove the dough from the work bowl, dust it with flour to coat, cut the dough into 4–6 pieces and, using your hands, flatten them into rectangles. Set the rollers of a manual pasta machine to the widest setting. Working with 1 piece at a time, crank the dough through the machine, dust with flour, fold it in half lengthwise and crank it through again. Continue to dust, fold and pass the dough through the machine until it feels smooth and satiny, 8–10 times.

The dough should feel considerably drier than when you started and look paler in color. Do not be afraid of over-handling the dough, it benefits from lots of rolling. Repeat with the other pieces. Cover the dough with a kitchen towel and let rest for 1 hour at room temperature to relax the gluten.

4. To store the dough, if desired, dust each piece with flour and place in a tightly covered container in the refrigerator for up to 1 week or in the freezer for up to 1 month. Bring to room temperature before proceeding.

5. To roll the dough, decrease the width of the roller opening by 1 notch. Working with 1 piece at a time, crank the dough through the machine twice. Reduce the roller opening by 1 notch and crank the dough through again. Continue reducing the roller opening and rolling the dough to the smallest setting on the machine, bearing in mind that pasta expands when cooked. Repeat with the other pieces.

6. Sprinkle a wooden board or a counter lined with waxed paper lightly with flour; do not work directly on laminate or tile to which pasta tends to stick. Place the pasta sheets side by side on the flour and let rest until they are dry to the touch but still pliant, about 10 minutes.

7. Cut the sheets according to the instructions beginning on page 14 or in the individual recipes.

Makes 1½ lb (750 g)

MAKING PASTA BY MACHINE:
STEP-BY-STEP

1. PROCESSING INGREDIENTS

Gather the pasta ingredients together (recipes on pages 10–11). In the work bowl of a food processor with the metal blade, combine all the ingredients. Pulse several times. Using a rubber spatula, scrape down the sides of the work bowl. Pulse quickly several times for a few seconds per pulse until the dough forms a soft ball.

2. KNEADING THE DOUGH

Dust with flour to coat and cut into pieces. Set the rollers of a manual pasta machine to the widest setting. Crank each piece through the machine, fold it in half lengthwise and crank through again. Continue to pass the dough through the machine, dusting as necessary, until it feels smooth and satiny.

3. ROLLING THE DOUGH

Decrease the rollers of the pasta machine by 1 setting. Crank each piece of dough through the machine twice. Continue reducing the roller opening, dusting as necessary and rolling the dough to the smallest setting on the machine.

4. PREPARING TO CUT

Sprinkle a wooden board or a counter lined with waxed paper lightly with flour. Place the pasta sheets on the flour and let rest until they are dry to the touch but still pliant, about 10 minutes. Cut the sheets according to the instructions in the individual recipes.

MAKING PASTA BY HAND

1. On a work surface, combine the semolina and all-purpose flours and salt in a mound. Make a well in the center and break in the eggs. Add water or flavoring ingredients. Using a fork, blend the ingredients in the well, gradually drawing in the flour and enlarging the well until all the ingredients are combined into a dough.

2. Dust a work surface with flour and transfer the dough to the surface. Using a dough scraper and the palm and heel of your hand, knead the dough, pushing it down and away from you and turning and folding it repeatedly, until the dough feels smooth and satiny, 7–10 minutes; sprinkle on extra flour any time the dough becomes sticky or soft during kneading. Cut the dough into pieces.

3. Place a piece of dough on a floured work surface. Using a floured rolling pin, roll the dough away from you, applying moderate pressure. Turn the dough over and around. Repeat, adding flour if the dough becomes sticky, until the pasta is $1/32$ inch (1 mm) thick for ribbons such as lasagne noodles and $1/64$ inch (.5 mm) thick for filled shapes. Repeat with the remaining dough.

4. Line a table or counter with waxed paper or kitchen towels and dust with flour. Place the pasta sheets on the paper or towels and let rest until they are dry to the touch but still pliant, about 10 minutes.

5. Cut the sheets according to the instructions in the individual recipes.

MAKING CRESPELLE

The Italian version of crepes, crespelle, are very easy to make once you get the hang of it. You'll need a 6-inch (15-cm) frying pan or crepe pan. Be sure to measure the bottom of the pan to ensure that it is the proper diameter. Most recipes for 6 people call for 12 crespelle. Remaining crespelle can be stacked, wrapped and frozen.

1 cup (5 oz/155 g) unbleached all-purpose (plain) flour

$3/4$ teaspoon salt

4 eggs, lightly beaten

2 cups (16 fl oz/500 ml) milk

6 tablespoons (3 fl oz/90 ml) pure olive oil

1. In a medium bowl, using a whisk or an electric mixer, mix the flour, salt, eggs, milk and 4 tablespoons (2 fl oz/60 ml) of the olive oil until smooth.

2. Coat a 6-inch (15-cm) frying pan with some of the remaining 2 tablespoons olive oil and heat it over medium-high heat. Add 2 tablespoons of the batter and distribute it evenly by swirling the pan quickly. Cook until the crespella is set, about 30 seconds. Using a narrow spatula, turn it over and cook for 5 seconds. Remove from the pan and place it on waxed paper. Repeat until all the batter has been used, adding more of the remaining olive oil to the pan as necessary. When the crespelle have cooled to room temperature, they may be stacked.

3. Use immediately or wrap in plastic and refrigerate for up to 3 days.

Makes 24 crespelle

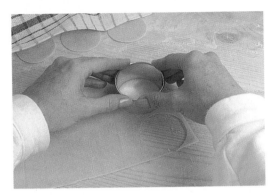

1. CUTTING THE ROUNDS

Make the fresh pasta and filling according to the individual recipes. Dust a wooden work surface with flour. Spread the pasta sheets on the surface (work in batches, if necessary). Using a round cookie cutter, cut the desired shapes. Place the rounds on waxed paper dusted with flour and cover with a kitchen towel. Cut twice the number of rounds as ravioli desired.

3. TOPPING THE ROUNDS

Top each round and filling with a reserved pasta round, carefully aligning the edges of the two. Brush the border with additional water, as necessary, to ensure that the two pieces of pasta stick together. Using your fingers, gently press the top round into the filling mound.

2. FILLING THE ROUNDS

Dust the work surface with flour. Place half the rounds on the surface (work in batches, if necessary). Using a pastry brush, lightly coat these rounds with water. Place about 1 teaspoon of filling in the center of each round, leaving a border on all sides.

4. SEALING THE ROUNDS

Using a fork, press the edges of the rounds together to secure the filling inside. Place the finished ravioli on waxed paper dusted with flour, cover with a kitchen towel and dry slightly before cooking, about 30 minutes.

MAKING SQUARE RAVIOLI: STEP-BY-STEP

1. TRIMMING THE SHEETS
Make the fresh pasta and filling according to the individual recipes. Dust a wooden work surface with flour. Spread two pasta sheets side-by-side on the surface. Using a knife and ruler, trim the pairs of pasta sheets to the exact same size. Repeat with additional pairs of sheets, if necessary.

3. TOPPING THE FILLING
Gently place the matching sheet of pasta directly over the first sheet, carefully aligning the edges of the two sheets. Using your fingers, gently press the top sheet around the filling mounds. Smooth the top sheet, pushing out any air bubbles.

2. PLACING THE FILLING
Using a pastry brush, lightly coat one sheet of pasta with water. Place about 1 teaspoon of filling in mounds approximately 2½ inches (6 cm) apart, leaving space around the outer edges of each mound.

4. CUTTING THE SQUARES
Using a ravioli cutter, fluted pastry wheel or knife and ruler, cut the sheets into individual squares. Check that the seal is secure. If there is a gap, use a fork to press the edges together. Place the ravioli on waxed paper dusted with flour, cover with a kitchen towel and dry slightly before cooking, about 30 minutes.

USING DRIED PASTA

Italian cooks do not think of dried pasta as lesser than fresh pasta. Instead, they think of them as two different yet equally delicious ingredients. As the recipes in this book vividly demonstrate, many different types of dried pasta may be used in baked and filled dishes. Those shown on the opposite page reflect just a small portion of the possibilities. By some estimates, there are more than 400 distinct commercial pasta shapes, inspired by centuries of imaginative cooks forming pasta by hand. Most pastas carry Italian names that fancifully describe these distinctive shapes. Unfortunately, all this creativity has resulted in some confusion: different manufacturers call similar shapes by different names. Further confusion comes into play when different shapes are called by the same name. The most important thing to remember when selecting, cooking and serving dried pasta is that the shapes are often interchangeable. If the type called for in a recipe is not available, simply use a pasta of similar size and shape.

DRIED SEMOLINA PASTA

The recipes in this book that call for dried pasta were designed and tested using semolina pasta. Dried semolina pasta is high in dietary fiber, low in fat, cholesterol-free and contains generous amounts of protein, making it a beneficial part of a balanced diet. Unlike pasta made from white flour, dried semolina pasta has a sturdier consistency that helps it maintain its chewy texture when immersed in boiling liquids or coated with a sauce. This sturdiness is especially important in baked dishes, when the pasta will be cooked twice, first boiled then baked.

Dried semolina pasta is manufactured entirely from hard (durum in Italian) wheat, a variety high in the elastic substance known as gluten, which gives pasta its desired sturdi-ness. Mixed with water, semolina flour forms a paste that is extruded through metal dies to make strands, ribbons, tubes or various other shapes. The pasta is then dried in chambers that carefully control humidity and temperature.

Dried semolina pasta may be labeled as containing hard-wheat, durum or semolina flour, which are simply different names for the same ingredient. By general consensus, Italian varieties are considered the best, but good varieties are now also being made elsewhere.

Dried pastas made from white flour can be used; their cooking times are usually shorter.

Once you have opened the package, store all dried pasta in tightly covered glass containers in a cool, dark place. Use within a year.

LASAGNE
12 minutes
cooking time

SPAGHETTINI
8 minutes
cooking time

ANGEL HAIR
4 minutes
cooking time

JUMBO SHELLS
8 minutes
cooking time

MANICOTTI
Muffs
12 minutes
cooking time

RADIATORI
Radiators
7 minutes
cooking time

FARFALLINE
Little Butterflies
2–3 minutes
cooking time

TUBETTI
Little Tubes
7 minutes
cooking time

ORZO
5–10 minutes
cooking time

PENNETTE
Little Quills
10–15 minutes
cooking time

COOKING PERFECT PASTA

If you can boil water and tell time, you can cook perfect pasta. No special skills or equipment are required, and the method is the same whether the pasta you're cooking is fresh or dried.

It is customary to add salt to the boiling water prior to adding the pasta. For the best taste, use kosher salt, which is slightly coarser in texture. It does not contain the anti-caking additives found in refined table salt and imparts more flavor. However, if you're following a special sodium-restricted diet, you can leave out the salt completely without adversely affecting the finished dish.

EQUIPMENT NEEDED

For the best results when cooking pasta, choose a two-handled pot large enough to allow the pasta to float freely while cooking. This will help prevent the pasta from sticking together. Use a long-handled slotted spoon or tongs to stir and lift the pasta as it cooks. A pasta fork, also called a pasta puller, is a long-handled plastic tool that looks like a spoon with a fluted edge; it is handy for lifting pasta shapes from the pot or serving bowl. Two thick pot holders or oven mitts and a sturdy colander that can withstand the heat of a large quantity of boiling water are also good investments for cooking pasta safely and successfully.

To ease cooking pasta in batches, consider investing in a special pasta pot, which includes a strainer insert that allows you to remove the pasta simply by lifting the insert from the pot (shown on the opposite page), eliminating the need for pouring the pasta and its cooking water into a colander.

AL DENTE OR TENDER

The Italian term "al dente" has become universally accepted as a description of perfectly cooked pasta. Translated as "to the tooth," it describes pasta that offers a slight resistance to the bite, being tender but still chewy in texture. Technically, al dente is used only to describe the perfectly cooked state of pasta that has been dried. Fresh pasta should be cooked just until "tender." In this case, tender means evenly soft but still chewy.

Either way, the best way to test for doneness is by biting into a single piece or strand of pasta. Use a slotted spoon or a long-handled cooking fork to fish it out of the boiling water.

Blow on the pasta briefly to cool it before biting into it. Dried pasta should be tender but firm and chewy. It should not show any white undercooked portion at its center; al dente does not mean underdone. Fresh pasta should taste cooked, without any taste of flour.

Ravioli and Lasagne

COOKING PASTA: STEP-BY-STEP

1. BOILING THE WATER
Shown here is a pasta pot with strainer insert. Use sufficient water in a large enough pot to allow the pasta to circulate freely. Over high heat, bring the water to a full, rolling boil. If desired, cover the pot to shorten the time needed to bring it to a boil.

3. BOILING THE PASTA
Cook the pasta, stirring occasionally, until it is al dente for dried, tender for fresh. Begin testing the pasta a minute or so before the earliest suggested time for doneness according to the recipes or the package directions.

2. ADDING SALT AND PASTA
When the water boils, add the salt. Adding the salt before the water boils may cause an unpleasant aftertaste. Shake off any excess flour from fresh pasta. Add the pasta, stirring to incorporate and prevent it from sticking.

4. DRAINING THE PASTA
Protecting your hands with pot holders or oven mitts, lift the strainer from the pot. Alternatively, carefully lift the pot and pour its contents into a colander placed in a sink. Lift and shake the strainer or colander until all the water has drained from the pasta.

Ravioli

SMOKED SALMON RAVIOLI WITH LEMON CREAM SAUCE

Serve these luxurious ravioli at an elegant supper. For an extra-special touch, garnish them not only with fresh chives but also with caviar or more reasonably priced orange-pink salmon roe.

1 lb (500 g) Black Pepper Pasta
   (recipe on page 10)

6 oz (185 g) sliced smoked salmon

1 tablespoon minced lemon zest

3 tablespoons sliced fresh chives
   Salt and freshly ground pepper

1 egg, lightly beaten

1 cup (8 oz/250 g) whole-milk
   ricotta cheese

⅓ cup (1½ oz/45 g) grated Parmesan
   cheese

6 qt (6 l) water

1 tablespoon salt

LEMON CREAM SAUCE

6 tablespoons (3 oz/90 g) crème
   fraîche or sour cream

1 tablespoon fresh lemon juice

1 teaspoon grated lemon zest

1 teaspoon minced fresh chives
   Salt and freshly ground pepper

1. Make the Black Pepper Pasta. Prepare the Lemon Cream Sauce (see below).
2. To make the filling, in a food processor with the metal blade or a blender, combine the salmon, lemon zest, 1 tablespoon of the chives and salt and pepper to taste. Pulse until the mixture is well combined but not fully smooth. Transfer to a medium bowl. Add the egg, ricotta cheese and Parmesan cheese. Stir to mix well. Cover and refrigerate for 1 hour.
3. Form the pasta and filling into thirty 3-inch (7.5-cm) round ravioli (see page 14).
4. In a large pot over high heat, bring the water to a boil. Add the 1 tablespoon salt and the ravioli in batches and cook until they rise to the surface, about 3 minutes, then cook for 1 minute more. Drain well.
5. To serve, divide among individual warmed plates. Top with an equal amount of the Lemon Cream Sauce and remaining chives.

LEMON CREAM SAUCE

1. In a medium bowl, whisk together the crème fraîche or sour cream, lemon juice, zest, chives and salt and pepper to taste. Serve at room temperature.

Serves 6

NUTRITIONAL ANALYSIS: Calories 368 (Kilojoules 1,545); Protein 20 g; Carbohydrates 42 g; Total Fat 13 g; Saturated Fat 6 g; Cholesterol 140 mg; Sodium 681 mg; Dietary Fiber 2 g

POTATO AND GARLIC RAVIOLI WITH BROWN BUTTER

This potato filling, rich with the flavors of garlic, chives and lemon juice, is also delicious served on its own as a side dish. The quantity of garlic may be reduced by half, if desired, and still yield a good flavor.

1 lb (500 g) Egg Pasta *(recipe on page 10)*

6 tablespoons (3 fl oz/90 ml) Brown Butter *(recipe on page 125)*

3 large russet potatoes

4 tablespoons (2 fl oz/60 ml) extra-virgin olive oil

6 garlic cloves, peeled and minced

3 tablespoons minced fresh chives

2 tablespoons fresh lemon juice
   Salt and freshly ground pepper

6 qt (6 l) water

1 tablespoon salt

1. Make the Egg Pasta and Brown Butter. Preheat an oven to 375°F (190°C).

2. Using a fork, puncture the potatoes in several places and bake until tender, about 45 minutes. Cool to the touch. Cut in half, scoop out the insides, place in a bowl and mash. Discard the skins.

3. To make the filling, in a small frying pan over medium heat, heat 1 tablespoon of the olive oil. Add the garlic and sauté for 1 minute. Add to the potatoes and stir to mix well. Add the remaining 3 tablespoons olive oil, 1 tablespoon of the chives, the lemon juice and salt and pepper to taste. Stir to mix well.

4. Form the pasta and filling into thirty-six 2½-inch (6-cm) round ravioli (see page 14).

5. In a large pot over high heat, bring the water to a boil. Add the 1 tablespoon salt and the ravioli in batches and cook until they rise to the surface, about 3 minutes, then cook for 1 minute more. Drain well.

6. To serve, divide among individual warmed plates. Top with an equal amount of melted Brown Butter and remaining chives.

Serves 6

NUTRITIONAL ANALYSIS: Calories 504 (Kilojoules 2,118); Protein 11 g; Carbohydrates 61 g; Total Fat 25 g; Saturated Fat 10 g; Cholesterol 104 mg; Sodium 379 mg; Dietary Fiber 4 g

THREE-CHEESE RAVIOLI WITH GREENS AND WALNUTS

The combination of cheeses and beaten egg produces a fluffy filling for vivid beet pasta. If you like, substitute fresh egg pasta. If fresh beet greens are hard to come by, use Swiss chard (silverbeet).

1   lb (500 g) Beet Pasta *(recipe on page 10)*
4   oz (125 g) whole-milk ricotta cheese
6   oz (185 g) fresh mild white goat cheese
1   cup (4 oz/125 g) grated pecorino romano cheese
2   eggs, lightly beaten
2   lb (1 kg) beet greens or chard, stemmed and cut into strips
3   tablespoons water, plus 6 qt (6 l) water
1   tablespoon salt
⅓   cup (3 fl oz/90 ml) extra-virgin olive oil
⅓   cup (1½ oz/45 g) walnut pieces, toasted *(see page 120)*

1. Make the Beet Pasta.
2. To make the filling, in a small bowl, combine the ricotta, goat and pecorino romano cheeses and eggs.
3. Form the pasta and filling into thirty-six 2½-inch (6-cm) square ravioli (see page 15).
4. In a heavy frying pan over medium heat, place the greens and the 3 tablespoons water, cover and cook until the greens wilt, about 5 minutes.
5. In a large pot over high heat, bring the 6 qt (6 l) water to a boil. Add the 1 tablespoon salt and the ravioli in batches and cook until they rise to the surface, about 3 minutes, then cook for 1 minute more. Drain well.
6. To serve, divide the wilted greens among individual warmed plates. Top with an equal amount of the ravioli, olive oil and walnuts.

Serves 6

NUTRITIONAL ANALYSIS: Calories 623 (Kilojoules 2,618); Protein 26 g; Carbohydrates 47 g; Total Fat 37 g; Saturated Fat 14 g; Cholesterol 193 mg; Sodium 1,234 mg; Dietary Fiber 2 g

Ravioli and Lasagne

TWO-TONED RAVIOLI WITH PESTO SAUCE

Form the ravioli one side Tomato Pasta and one side Spinach Pasta for a lovely presentation. Make 1 lb (500 g) of each pasta and, after kneading, store the extra in a tightly covered container in the refrigerator for up to 1 week.

8 oz (250 g) Tomato Pasta *(recipe on page 10)*

8 oz (250 g) Spinach Pasta *(recipe on page 10)*

1 cup (8 fl oz/250 ml) Pesto Sauce *(recipe on page 127)*

3 oz (90 g) ricotta cheese

4 oz (125 g) fresh mild white goat cheese at room temperature

2 oz (60 g) Parmesan cheese, grated

6 qt (6 l) water

1 tablespoon salt

2 tomatoes, peeled, seeded and chopped *(see page 122)*

2 tablespoons pine nuts, toasted *(see page 120)*

1. Make the Tomato Pasta, Spinach Pasta and Pesto Sauce.
2. To make the filling, in a medium bowl, combine the ricotta, goat and Parmesan cheeses and ¼ cup (2 fl oz/ 60 ml) of the Pesto Sauce. Stir to mix well.
3. Form the pastas and filling into thirty-six 2½-inch (6-cm) square ravioli (see page 15).
4. In a large pot over high heat, bring the water to a boil. Add the 1 tablespoon salt and the ravioli in batches and cook until they rise to the surface, about 3 minutes, then cook for 1 minute more. Drain well and place on a large warmed platter.
5. In a small bowl, thin the remaining Pesto Sauce with 3 tablespoons of the pasta cooking water. Add half of the thinned Pesto to the ravioli and toss gently.
6. To serve, divide among individual warmed plates. Top with an equal amount of the remaining thinned Pesto Sauce, tomatoes and pine nuts.

Serves 6

NUTRITIONAL ANALYSIS: Calories 664 (Kilojoules 2,789); Protein 24 g; Carbohydrates 50 g; Total Fat 43 g; Saturated Fat 15 g; Cholesterol 121 mg; Sodium 1,075 mg; Dietary Fiber 3 g

CURRIED-POTATO AND PEA RAVIOLI WITH YOGURT SAUCE

The filling for these ravioli was inspired by one used in samosa, *traditional deep-fried Indian vegetarian turnovers. If you like, substitute other vegetables such as carrots or zucchini (courgettes), diced, for all or some of the peas.*

1 lb (500 g) Saffron Pasta *(recipe on page 10)*

¼ cup (2 fl oz/60 ml) Clarified Butter *(recipe on page 123)*

2 russet potatoes

1 cup (5 oz/155 g) shelled fresh peas or frozen peas, thawed

½ yellow onion, peeled and diced

1 tablespoon curry powder

1 teaspoon ground cumin

½ teaspoon ground turmeric

¼ teaspoon ground cardamom

Cayenne pepper

Salt

1 tablespoon unsalted butter

2 teaspoons curry powder

¾ cup (6 oz/185 g) plain yogurt

6 qt (6 l) water

1 tablespoon salt

6 tablespoons (1½ oz/45 g) Major Grey's chutney

1. Make the Saffron Pasta and Clarified Butter. Preheat an oven to 375°F (190°C).

2. Using a fork, puncture the potatoes in several places and bake until tender, about 45 minutes. Cool to the touch. Cut in half, scrape out the insides, place in a medium bowl and mash. Discard the skins.

3. In a small saucepan of boiling salted water, cook the peas until just tender, about 4 minutes. Drain well.

4. To make the filling, in a small frying pan over low heat, heat the Clarified Butter. Add the onion and sauté, stirring frequently, until tender and fragrant, about 15 minutes. Add the curry, cumin, turmeric, cardamom and cayenne and salt to taste and cook for 2 minutes. Add to the potatoes. Add the peas and stir to mix well.

5. Form the pasta and filling into thirty-six 2½-inch (6-cm) round ravioli (see page 14).

6. To make the yogurt sauce, in a small saucepan over medium-low heat, melt the butter until it foams. Stir in the curry and cook, stirring continuously, for 2 minutes. Reduce the heat to low, add the yogurt and stir until it is just warmed through.

7. In a large pot over high heat, bring the water to a boil. Add the 1 tablespoon salt and the ravioli in batches and cook until they rise to the surface, about 3 minutes, then cook for 1 minute more. Drain well.

8. To serve, divide among individual warmed plates. Top with an equal amount of the yogurt sauce and chutney.

Serves 6

NUTRITIONAL ANALYSIS: Calories 420 (Kilojoules 1,766); Protein 12 g; Carbohydrates 61 g; Total Fat 14 g; Saturated Fat 8 g; Cholesterol 102 mg; Sodium 454 mg; Dietary Fiber 5 g

LEMON RAVIOLI WITH PUMPKIN FILLING

Serve these festive ravioli, based on a traditional Italian recipe, for the winter holidays. A hint of cinnamon may be added to the mixture, or substitute a dash of commercial pumpkin pie spice blend for the nutmeg and cloves.

1 lb (500 g) Lemon Pasta *(recipe on page 10)*

2 cups (16 fl oz/500 ml) pumpkin purée

2 tablespoons candied ginger, minced

2 tablespoons candied lemon peel, minced

3 tablespoons currants, soaked in brandy or water for 30 minutes and drained

1 tablespoon white mustard seed

Salt and freshly ground pepper

Ground nutmeg

Ground cloves

6 qt (6 l) water

1 tablespoon salt

6 tablespoons (3 oz/90 g) unsalted butter at room temperature

6 tablespoons (1½ oz/45 g) grated Parmesan cheese

1. Make the Lemon Pasta.
2. To make the filling, in a medium bowl, combine the pumpkin, ginger, lemon peel, currants, mustard seed and salt, pepper, nutmeg and cloves to taste. Stir to mix well.
3. Form the pasta and filling into thirty 3-inch (7.5-cm) round ravioli (see page 14).
4. In a large pot over high heat, bring the water to a boil. Add the 1 tablespoon salt and the ravioli in batches and cook until they rise to the surface, about 3 minutes, then cook for 1 minute more. Drain well and place on a large warmed platter. Top with half of the butter and toss gently.
5. To serve, divide among individual warmed plates. Top with an equal amount of the remaining butter and the Parmesan cheese.

Serves 6

NUTRITIONAL ANALYSIS: Calories 416 (Kilojoules 1,748); Protein 12 g; Carbohydrates 55 g; Total Fat 16 g; Saturated Fat 9 g; Cholesterol 107 mg; Sodium 582 mg; Dietary Fiber 2 g

CRAB RAVIOLI WITH HOT LEMON BUTTER SAUCE

When preparing ravioli seems too time-consuming, use this crab filling for cannelloni made with the same fresh pasta dough or in dried manicotti and serve with the same sauce.

1 lb (500 g) Lemon Pasta *(recipe on page 10)*

1 tablespoon unsalted butter

¼ cup (1½ oz/45 g) minced onion

½ cup (2½ oz/75 g) finely diced celery

9 oz (280 g) fresh crabmeat

2 teaspoons Dijon-style mustard

2 tablespoons heavy (double) cream

1 egg, lightly beaten

2 tablespoons fresh lemon juice

2 tablespoons minced fresh flat-leaf (Italian) parsley

¼ cup (½ oz/15 g) dried bread crumbs *(see page 116)*

Salt

Red pepper flakes

6 qt (6 l) water

1 tablespoon salt

1 lemon, cut into 6 slices

HOT LEMON BUTTER

½ cup (4 oz/125 g) unsalted butter

4 garlic cloves, peeled and minced

1 tablespoon fresh lemon juice

2 teaspoons hot pepper sauce

1 teaspoon grated lemon zest

1. Make the Lemon Pasta. Prepare the Hot Lemon Butter (see below).

2. In a small frying pan over medium-low heat, melt the butter until it foams. Reduce the heat to low, add the onion and celery and sauté, stirring frequently, until tender, about 15 minutes.

3. To make the filling, in a medium bowl, combine the crabmeat, mustard, cream, egg, lemon juice, parsley, bread crumbs and salt and red pepper flakes to taste. Add the sautéed onion and celery and toss to mix well.

4. Form the pasta and filling into thirty-six 2½-inch (6-cm) square ravioli (see page 15).

5. In a large pot over high heat, bring the water to a boil. Add the 1 tablespoon salt and the ravioli in batches and cook until they rise to the surface, about 3 minutes, then cook for 1 minute more. Drain well.

6. To serve, divide among individual warmed plates. Top with an equal amount of the Hot Lemon Butter and garnish with a lemon slice.

HOT LEMON BUTTER

1. In a small saucepan over medium-low heat, melt the butter and skim off the foam that forms on top. Add the garlic and simmer for 2 minutes. Stir in the lemon juice, hot pepper sauce and lemon zest. Reheat before serving.

Serves 6

NUTRITIONAL ANALYSIS: Calories 465 (Kilojoules 1,951); Protein 19 g; Carbohydrates 45 g; Total Fat 23 g; Saturated Fat 13 g; Cholesterol 202 mg; Sodium 712 mg; Dietary Fiber 2 g

 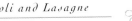

Turkey and Sage Ravioli with Sage Cream Sauce

The natural affinity between turkey and sage produces an especially flavorful pasta filling. If you cannot locate the fresh herb, substitute 1 tablespoon of dried but not ground sage.

1 lb (500 g) Egg Pasta *(recipe on page 10)*

3 tablespoons olive oil

1 yellow onion, peeled and finely chopped

1 shallot, peeled and minced

1 celery stalk, finely chopped

1 lb (500 g) ground (minced) turkey

2 tablespoons minced fresh sage
Salt and freshly ground pepper

6 qt (6 l) water

1 tablespoon salt
Fresh sage sprigs

Sage Cream Sauce

2 tablespoons unsalted butter

1 shallot, peeled and minced

2 tablespoons minced fresh sage

2 cups (16 fl oz/500 ml) heavy (double) cream

3 fresh sage sprigs
Salt and freshly ground pepper

1. Make the Egg Pasta. Prepare the Sage Cream Sauce (see below).
2. To make the filling, in a large, heavy frying pan over medium heat, heat the olive oil. Add the onion, shallot and celery and cook until they are tender, about 15 minutes. Add the turkey and cook, breaking it up with a fork, until it is no longer pink. Add the minced sage and salt and pepper to taste. Stir to mix well. Cool to room temperature.
3. Form the pasta and filling into thirty-six 2½-inch (6-cm) square ravioli (see page 15).
4. In a large pot over high heat, bring the water to a boil. Add the 1 tablespoon salt and the ravioli in batches and cook until they rise to the surface, about 3 minutes, then cook for 1 minute more. Drain well.
5. To serve, divide among individual warmed plates. Top with the Sage Cream Sauce and garnish with a sage sprig.

Sage Cream Sauce

1. In a small saucepan over medium-low heat, melt the butter until it foams. Add the shallot and minced sage and sauté until the shallot is tender, about 5 minutes. Add the cream and sage sprigs and simmer until the cream is reduced by half, about 15 minutes. Cool for 10 minutes. Remove and discard the sage sprigs.
2. Strain the sauce into a clean saucepan and add salt and pepper to taste. Reheat before serving.

Serves 6

Nutritional Analysis: Calories 702 (Kilojoules 2,950); Protein 24 g; Carbohydrates 44 g; Total Fat 48 g; Saturated Fat 24 g; Cholesterol 245 mg; Sodium 479 mg; Dietary Fiber 2 g

PORK AND DRIED APRICOT RAVIOLI WITH APRICOT AND WINE SAUCE

Sweet apricots find a perfect flavor counterpoint in both this pork filling and spiced wine sauce. Using the dried version in the filling and jam in the sauce brings a taste of summer to a dish you can make any time of year.

1	lb (500 g) Egg Pasta *(recipe on page 10)*
3	tablespoons olive oil
1	yellow onion, peeled and finely diced
5	garlic cloves, peeled and minced
1	lb (500 g) ground (minced) pork
¾	cup (3 oz/90 g) dried apricots, finely diced
6	tablespoons (2 oz/60 g) pine nuts, toasted *(see page 120)*
	Salt
	Ground cumin
	Ground cinnamon
	Ground cloves
6	qt (6 l) water
1	tablespoon salt

APRICOT AND WINE SAUCE

2	tablespoons olive oil
1	small yellow onion, peeled and minced
4	garlic cloves, peeled and minced
1	teaspoon minced fresh ginger
½	cup (5 oz/155 g) apricot jam
1½	cups (12 fl oz/375 g) dry white wine
	Ground cloves
	Ground nutmeg
	Ground cinnamon

1. Make the Egg Pasta. Prepare the Apricot and Wine Sauce (see below).

2. To make the filling, in a medium frying pan over medium heat, heat the olive oil. Add the onion and sauté, stirring frequently, until tender and fragrant, about 15 minutes. Add the garlic and sauté for 2 minutes. Add the pork and cook, breaking it up with a fork, until it is no longer pink, about 5 minutes. Drain off any excess fat and return the pan to the heat. Add the apricots, half the pine nuts and salt, cumin, cinnamon and cloves to taste. Stir to mix well.

3. Form the pasta and filling into thirty 3-inch (7.5-cm) round ravioli (see page 14).

4. In a large pot over high heat, bring the water to a boil. Add the 1 tablespoon salt and the ravioli in batches and cook until they rise to the surface, about 3 minutes, then cook for 1 minute more. Drain well.

5. To serve, divide among individual warmed plates. Top with an equal amount of the Apricot and Wine Sauce and remaining pine nuts.

APRICOT AND WINE SAUCE

1. In a small frying pan, heat the olive oil over medium heat. Add the onion and sauté, stirring frequently, until the onion is transparent, about 10 minutes. Add the garlic and sauté for 2 minutes. Add the ginger, jam, wine and cloves, nutmeg and cinnamon to taste. Stir to mix well. Simmer until the sauce is fragrant, about 15 minutes. Reheat before serving.

Serves 6

NUTRITIONAL ANALYSIS: Calories 723 (Kilojoules 3,037); Protein 25 g; Carbohydrates 72 g; Total Fat 34 g; Saturated Fat 9 g; Cholesterol 125 mg; Sodium 430 mg; Dietary Fiber 5 g

Ravioli and Lasagne

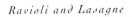

CHICKEN RAVIOLI WITH MARSALA CREAM SAUCE

The filling for these ravioli resembles fresh chicken sausage. If you can find them, feel free to use them in place of the filling mixture, removing the casing and sautéing the mixture for about 5 minutes.

1 lb (500 g) Egg Pasta *(recipe on page 10)*

3 tablespoons olive oil

1 yellow onion, peeled and finely diced

1 pippin apple, peeled, cored and finely diced

1 lb (500 g) ground (minced) chicken

1 tablespoon curry powder

Ground cardamom

2 cups (16 fl oz/500 ml) half & half (half cream)

2 tablespoons unsalted butter

2 tablespoons minced onion

1 tablespoon curry powder

Ground cardamom

¾ cup (6 fl oz/180 ml) dry Marsala wine

Salt

Cayenne pepper

6 qt (6 l) water

1 tablespoon salt

1. Make the Egg Pasta.

2. To make the filling, in a medium frying pan over medium heat, heat the olive oil. Add the onion and sauté, stirring frequently, until tender and fragrant, about 15 minutes. Add the apple and chicken, breaking it up with a fork, and cook until the chicken is no longer pink, about 5 minutes. Add the curry and cardamom to taste. Stir to mix well.

3. Form the pasta and filling into thirty-six 2½-inch (6-cm) round ravioli (see page 14).

4. To make the Marsala cream sauce, in a medium saucepan over medium heat, cook the half & half to reduce by one-third, 12–15 minutes. In a small frying pan over medium heat, melt the butter until it foams. Reduce the heat to medium-low, add the onion and sauté, stirring frequently, until fragrant, about 10 minutes. Add the curry and cardamom to taste and cook for 2 minutes.

5. Increase the heat to medium, stir in the wine and simmer until it is reduced to 3 tablespoons, about 15 minutes. Reduce the heat to medium-low, add the reduced half & half and simmer for 5 minutes. Add salt and cayenne to taste. Keep warm.

6. In a large pot over high heat, bring the water to a boil. Add the 1 tablespoon salt and the ravioli in batches and cook until they rise to the surface, about 3 minutes, then cook for 1 minute more. Drain well.

7. To serve, divide among individual warmed plates. Top with an equal amount of the wine sauce.

Serves 6

NUTRITIONAL ANALYSIS: Calories 597 (Kilojoules 2,509); Protein 25 g; Carbohydrates 51 g; Total Fat 29 g; Saturated Fat 11 g; Cholesterol 174 mg; Sodium 469 mg; Dietary Fiber 3 g

Ravioli

WILD RICE RAVIOLI WITH WALNUT BUTTER SAUCE

Though it may seem unusual to fill pasta with rice, these festive ravioli, full of autumn flavors, make a perfect first course before a holiday turkey or ham.

1 lb (500 g) Egg Pasta *(recipe on page 10)*

½ cup (3 oz/90 g) wild rice

2 cups (16 fl oz/500 ml) water

1 teaspoon plus 1 tablespoon salt

¾ cup (3 oz/90 g) chopped walnuts, toasted *(see page 120)*

¼ cup (1 oz/30 g) dried cranberries, soaked in warm water for 30 minutes and drained

3 tablespoons minced fresh flat-leaf (Italian) parsley

2 tablespoons unsalted butter, melted
   Freshly ground pepper

6 qt (6 l) water

WALNUT BUTTER SAUCE

⅓ cup (3 oz/90 g) unsalted butter

¼ cup (1 oz/30 g) grated Parmesan cheese

¼ cup (1 oz/30 g) chopped walnuts, toasted *(see page 120)*

1 tablespoon minced fresh flat-leaf (Italian) parsley
   Salt and freshly ground pepper

1. Make the Egg Pasta. Prepare the Walnut Butter Sauce (see below).

2. In a small saucepan over medium heat, combine the rice, water and the 1 teaspoon salt and bring to a boil. Reduce the heat to medium-low, cover and cook until the rice is tender, about 40 minutes. Drain any excess water.

3. To make the filling, in a medium bowl, combine the rice, walnuts, cranberries and parsley. Toss to mix well. Add the butter and pepper to taste and toss again.

4. Form the pasta and filling into thirty 3-inch (7.5-cm) square ravioli (see page 15).

5. In a large pot over high heat, bring the water to a boil. Add the 1 tablespoon salt and the ravioli in batches and cook until they rise to the surface, about 3 minutes, then cook for 1 minute more. Drain well and place on a large warmed platter. Top with half of the Walnut Butter Sauce. Toss to coat well.

6. To serve, divide among individual warmed plates. Top with an equal amount of the remaining Walnut Butter Sauce.

WALNUT BUTTER SAUCE

1. In a small saucepan over low heat, melt the butter. Add the Parmesan cheese, walnuts and parsley and salt and pepper to taste. Stir to mix well. Reheat before serving.

Serves 6

NUTRITIONAL ANALYSIS: Calories 544 (Kilojoules 2,286); Protein 15 g; Carbohydrates 56 g; Total Fat 29 g; Saturated Fat 11 g; Cholesterol 112 mg; Sodium 831 mg; Dietary Fiber 4 g

$\mathscr{S}$PINACH RAVIOLI WITH SUMMER TOMATO SAUCE

This classic dish features both ricotta and Parmesan cheeses mixed with spinach as a filling for round ravioli. They are topped with a simple tomato purée that is also delicious on pasta noodles.

1	lb (500 g) Egg Pasta *(recipe on page 10)*
1¾	cups (14 fl oz/435 ml) Summer Tomato Sauce *(recipe on page 127)*
2	tablespoons extra-virgin olive oil
4	garlic cloves, peeled and minced
2	lb (1 kg) fresh spinach, stemmed and chopped
1	teaspoon minced lemon zest
½	cup (4 oz/125 g) ricotta cheese
½	cup (4 oz/125 g) freshly grated Parmesan cheese
	Salt
6	qt (6 l) water
1	tablespoon salt

1. Make the Egg Pasta and Summer Tomato Sauce.

2. To make the filling, in a small frying pan over medium-low heat, heat the olive oil. Add the garlic and sauté for 1 minute. Add the spinach, cover and cook until the spinach is wilted, 3–4 minutes. Cool to room temperature and add the lemon zest, ricotta and Parmesan cheeses and salt to taste. Stir to mix well.

3. Form the pasta and filling into thirty-six 2½-inch (6-cm) round ravioli (see page 14).

4. In a large pot over high heat bring the water to a boil. Add the 1 tablespoon salt and the ravioli in batches and cook until they rise to the surface, about 3 minutes, then cook for 1 minute more. Drain well.

5. To serve, divide among individual warmed plates. Top with an equal amount of the Summer Tomato Sauce.

Serves 6

NUTRITIONAL ANALYSIS: Calories 509 (Kilojoules 2,137); Protein 19 g; Carbohydrates 56 g; Total Fat 25 g; Saturated Fat 12 g; Cholesterol 119 mg; Sodium 648 mg; Dietary Fiber 8 g

Ravioli

Lasagne and Baked Pastas

$\mathscr{B}$OLOGNESE LASAGNE

Although many different kinds of Italian lasagne may be found, this version is undoubtedly a classic with its simple layers of noodles, meaty sauce and cheese.

4	cups (32 fl oz/1 l) Bolognese Sauce *(recipe on page 124)*
6	qt (6 l) water
1	tablespoon salt
18	dried lasagne noodles
1½	cups (6 oz/185 g) grated pecorino romano cheese
¼	cup (⅓ oz/10 g) minced fresh flat-leaf (Italian) parsley

1. Make the Bolognese Sauce. Preheat an oven to 350°F (180°C). Coat the inside of a 9-x13-inch (23-x33-cm) baking dish with olive oil.

2. In a large pot over high heat, bring the water to a boil. Add the 1 tablespoon salt and the lasagne noodles and cook according to the package directions or until al dente (see page 18), about 12 minutes. Drain well, rinse in cool water and drain again.

3. Cover the bottom of the baking dish with 3 lasagne noodles, touching but not overlapping. Make 6 layers of the Bolognese Sauce, pecorino romano cheese and noodles, ending with the cheese. Top with the parsley. Bake until the top is golden brown and the sauce is bubbling, 35–45 minutes.

4. To serve, cool for 10 minutes and divide among individual warmed plates.

Serves 8

NUTRITIONAL ANALYSIS: Calories 549 (Kilojoules 2,305); Protein 24 g; Carbohydrates 52 g; Total Fat 25 g; Saturated Fat 10 g; Cholesterol 67 mg; Sodium 1,299 mg; Dietary Fiber 3 g

TOMATO, ANCHOVY AND ARTICHOKE HEART LASAGNE

This variation on layered and baked lasagne features artichoke hearts highlighted by tomatoes, garlic and pungent anchovies. If you have the time, make the dish with fresh Lemon Pasta (recipe on page 10).

2　tablespoons unsalted butter

¼　cup (2 fl oz/60 ml) extra-virgin olive oil

1¼　lb (625 g) yellow onions, chopped

1　tablespoon minced garlic

5　anchovy fillets, drained and diced

2　tomatoes, peeled, seeded and diced *(see page 122)*

　　Salt and freshly ground pepper

6　qt (6 l) water

1　tablespoon salt

15　dried lasagne noodles

6　frozen artichoke hearts, thawed and cut into thin strips

4　cups (1 lb/500 g) grated Fontina cheese

　　Fresh flat-leaf (Italian) parsley sprigs

1. Preheat an oven to 350°F (180°C). Coat the inside of a 9-x13-inch (23-x33-cm) baking dish with olive oil.

2. In a medium frying pan over medium-low heat, heat the butter and olive oil until the butter is melted. Add the onions, reduce the heat to low and sauté, stirring frequently, until the onions are tender and fragrant, about 15 minutes. Add the garlic and anchovies and sauté for 2 minutes. Add the tomatoes and simmer for 10 minutes. Add salt and pepper to taste. Stir to mix well.

3. In a large pot over high heat, bring the water to a boil. Add the 1 tablespoon salt and the lasagne noodles and cook according to the package directions or until al dente (see page 18), about 12 minutes. Drain well, rinse in cool water and drain again.

4. Cover the bottom of the baking dish with 3 lasagne noodles, touching but not overlapping. Make 5 layers of the tomato mixture, artichoke strips, Fontina cheese and noodles, ending with the cheese. Bake until the top is golden brown and the sauce is bubbling, 30–35 minutes.

5. To serve, cool for 10 minutes and divide among individual warmed plates. Garnish with a parsley sprig.

Serves 6

NUTRITIONAL ANALYSIS: Calories 720 (Kilojoules 3,023); Protein 31 g; Carbohydrates 62 g; Total Fat 39 g; Saturated Fat 19 g; Cholesterol 100 mg; Sodium 975 mg; Dietary Fiber 5 g

Lasagne and Baked Pastas

FRESH LASAGNE WITH BASIL AND BÉCHAMEL SAUCE

Try this aromatic dish in summer or fall, when fresh basil is most abundant. For a satisfying vegetarian meal, accompany it with crusty bread and a platter of sun-ripened sliced tomatoes topped with fresh basil leaves.

3 cups (24 fl oz/750 ml) Béchamel Sauce *(recipe on page 124)*

1½ lb (750 g) Egg Pasta *(recipe on page 11)*

4 cups (4 oz/125 g) packed fresh basil leaves

8 garlic cloves, peeled and chopped

¾ cup (4 oz/125 g) pine nuts, lightly toasted *(see page 120)*

 Salt

⅔ cup (5 fl oz/160 ml) extra-virgin olive oil

6 qt (6 l) water

1 tablespoon salt

1½ cups (6 oz/185 g) grated pecorino romano cheese

 Fresh basil sprigs

1. Make the Béchamel Sauce and Egg Pasta. Preheat an oven to 375°F (190°C). Coat the inside of a 9-x13-inch (23-x33-cm) baking dish with olive oil.

2. To make the lasagne noodles, using a fluted pastry wheel, cut the pasta sheets into 12 ribbons about 2½ inches (6 cm) wide and 12 inches (30 cm) long. Dry 15–30 minutes before cooking.

3. In a food processor with the metal blade or a blender, mince the basil and garlic. Add ½ cup (2½ oz/75 g) of the pine nuts and salt to taste and pulse several times. With the motor running, add the olive oil in a steady stream.

4. In a large pot over high heat, bring the water to a boil. Add the 1 tablespoon salt and the lasagne noodles and cook until tender (see page 18), about 2½ minutes. Drain well.

5. In a medium bowl, combine the basil mixture, 1 cup (4 oz/125 g) of the pecorino romano cheese and the Béchamel Sauce. Stir to mix well. Spread ¼ cup (3 fl oz/90 ml) into the baking dish. Cover with 3 lasagne noodles, touching but not overlapping. Make 6 layers of the basil and Béchamel mixture and noodles, ending with the basil and Béchamel mixture. Top with the remaining pecorino romano cheese and pine nuts. Bake until the top is just beginning to brown, 12–15 minutes.

6. To serve, cool for 10 minutes and divide among individual warmed plates. Garnish with a basil sprig.

Serves 8

NUTRITIONAL ANALYSIS: Calories 704 (Kilojoules 2,955); Protein 18 g; Carbohydrates 41 g; Total Fat 53 g; Saturated Fat 20 g; Cholesterol 139 mg; Sodium 889 mg; Dietary Fiber 3 g

CARAMELIZED ONION AND PANCETTA LASAGNE

With its hearty ingredients, this lasagne works best when made with dried noodles. If possible, make this casserole a few hours before baking and serving to give the flavors time to marry. Prosciutto may replace the pancetta.

3 cups (24 fl oz/750 ml) Béchamel Sauce *(recipe on page 124)*

4 cups (14 oz/420 g) Caramelized Onions *(recipe on page 126)*

6 qt (6 l) water

1 tablespoon salt

15 dried lasagne noodles

1 tablespoon olive oil

8 oz (250 g) pancetta, minced

12 oz (375 g) fresh mozzarella cheese, thinly sliced

Fresh flat-leaf (Italian) parsley sprigs

1. Make the Béchamel Sauce and Caramelized Onions. Preheat an oven to 350°F (180°C). Coat the inside of a 9-x13-inch (23-x33-cm) baking dish with olive oil.
2. In a large pot over high heat, bring the water to a boil. Add the 1 tablespoon salt and the lasagne noodles and cook according to the package directions or until al dente (see page 18), about 12 minutes. Drain well, rinse in cool water and drain again. Immediately toss with the olive oil.
3. Spread ¼ cup (2 fl oz/60 ml) of the Béchamel Sauce in the bottom of the baking dish. Cover with 3 lasagne noodles, touching but not overlapping. Make 5 layers of the Caramelized Onions, pancetta, mozzarella cheese and noodles, ending with the cheese. Top with the remaining Béchamel Sauce. Cover tightly with aluminum foil and bake for 30 minutes. Remove the foil and bake until the top is just beginning to brown, about 10 minutes longer.
4. To serve, cool for 10 minutes and divide among individual warmed plates. Garnish with a parsley sprig.

Serves 6

NUTRITIONAL ANALYSIS: Calories 836 (Kilojoules 3,513); Protein 24 g; Carbohydrates 67 g; Total Fat 53 g; Saturated Fat 24 g; Cholesterol 145 mg; Sodium 728 mg; Dietary Fiber 5 g

PENNETTE AND BEAN SOUP WITH A CHEESE CRUST

A variation on pasta e fagioli, *Italy's traditional pasta-and-bean soup, this robust dish is ideal served as the first course of a winter dinner — or as a main dish in its own right, accompanied with salad and bread.*

8   oz (250 g) dried cannellini beans, soaked 3 hours to overnight in water

3   tablespoons olive oil

2   cups (8 oz/250 g) diced yellow onions

2   tablespoons minced garlic

4   oz (125 g) pancetta, finely chopped

2   tomatoes, peeled, seeded and diced *(see page 122)*

6   cups (48 fl oz/1.5 l) canned reduced-sodium beef stock

¼   cup (⅓ oz/10 g) minced fresh flat-leaf (Italian) parsley

2   tablespoons minced fresh oregano

4   qt (4 l) water

2   teaspoons salt

8   oz (250 g) dried pennette
     Salt and freshly ground pepper

6   slices country bread, toasted

3   cups (12 oz/375 g) grated Fontina cheese

1. Preheat an oven to 350°F (180°C).
2. Drain the cannellini beans, place in a medium pot with water to cover. Cook, uncovered, over medium heat until almost tender, 30–35 minutes. Drain well.
3. In a heavy frying pan over medium heat, heat the olive oil. Add the onions, reduce the heat to low and sauté, stirring frequently, until tender and fragrant, about 15 minutes. Add the garlic and sauté for 2 minutes. Add the pancetta and sauté for 5 minutes. Add the tomatoes, beef stock, parsley, oregano and cooked beans and simmer for 10 minutes.
4. In a large pot over high heat, bring the 4 qt (4 l) water to a boil. Add the 2 teaspoons salt and the pennette and cook according to the package directions or until almost al dente (see page 18), about 9 minutes. Drain well and add to the bean mixture. Add salt and pepper to taste.
5. To serve, ladle the soup into individual ovenproof bowls, leaving at least ½ inch (12 mm) of room at the top. Top with 1 piece of bread and an equal amount of the Fontina cheese, spreading it on the surface of the bread. Place on a baking sheet and bake until the cheese is completely melted, about 10 minutes.

Serves 6

NUTRITIONAL ANALYSIS: Calories 815 (Kilojoules 3,424); Protein 43 g; Carbohydrates 75 g; Total Fat 39 g; Saturated Fat 18 g; Cholesterol 99 mg; Sodium 1,753 mg; Dietary Fiber 7 g

RZO IN TOMATO BROTH WITH A CHEESE CRUST

Orzo is a small seed-shaped pasta made from barley. Other small-shaped pastas or rice can be substituted in this hearty soup. The creamy melted cheese crust provides an unusual presentation.

5 qt (5 l) water

1 tablespoon salt

12 oz (375 g) orzo

2 tablespoons olive oil

1 small red (Spanish) onion, peeled and cut lengthwise into thin strips

1 tablespoon minced garlic

4 cups (32 fl oz/1 l) Chicken Stock (*recipe on page 125*)

4 tomatoes, peeled, seeded and diced (*see page 122*)

3 tablespoons minced fresh flat-leaf (Italian) parsley

Salt and freshly ground pepper

3 cups (12 oz/375 g) grated Fontina cheese

1. Preheat an oven to 325°F (165°C).

2. In a large pot over high heat, bring the water to a boil. Add the 1 tablespoon salt and the orzo and cook according to the package directions or until almost al dente (see page 18), 5–10 minutes. Drain well and place in a large bowl.

3. In a medium pot over medium heat, heat the olive oil. Add the onion and sauté, stirring frequently, until soft, about 5 minutes. Add the garlic and sauté for 2 minutes. Add the Chicken Stock and tomatoes, reduce the heat to medium-low and simmer for 8 minutes. Add the parsley, orzo and salt and pepper to taste. Stir to mix well.

4. To serve, ladle the soup into individual ovenproof bowls. Top with an equal amount of the Fontina cheese. Place on a baking sheet and bake until the cheese is fully melted and the soup is steaming hot, about 10 minutes.

Serves 6

NUTRITIONAL ANALYSIS: Calories 520 (Kilojoules 2,182); Protein 25 g; Carbohydrates 52 g; Total Fat 25 g; Saturated Fat 12 g; Cholesterol 66 mg; Sodium 740 mg; Dietary Fiber 3 g

Lasagne and Baked Pastas

ORZO WITH WINTER SQUASH AND LEEKS

Any winter squash, including sugar pumpkin, Delicata or butternut squash, will work well in this comforting dish. Use a slightly larger pasta, such as farfalline or small shells, if you cannot locate orzo. Serve with a simple salad.

1　lb (500 g) squash, seeded and cut into large pieces

　Cayenne pepper

　Ground nutmeg

　Freshly ground pepper

4　qt (4 l) water

2　teaspoons salt

12　oz (375 g) dried orzo

3　tablespoons olive oil

2　oz (60 g) pancetta, finely chopped

2　tablespoons unsalted butter

2　leeks, white parts and 2 inches (5 cm) green parts, thinly sliced

1　cup (4 oz/125 g) dried bread crumbs *(see page 116)*

¾　cup (3 oz/90 g) grated pecorino romano cheese

　Salt

2　cups (16 fl oz/500 ml) Chicken Stock *(see page 125)*

1. Preheat an oven to 325°F (165°C). Thinly coat a baking sheet with olive oil.

2. Place the squash on the baking sheet, cut side down, and bake until the squash is soft and tender, about 45 minutes. Cool to the touch, remove the pulp, place in a small bowl and mash. Discard the skins. Add the cayenne, nutmeg and pepper to taste.

3. In a large pot over high heat, bring the water to a boil. Add the 2 teaspoons salt and the orzo and cook according to the package directions or until al dente (see page 18), 5–10 minutes. Drain well, rinse in cool water, drain again, place in a bowl and immediately toss with 1 tablespoon of the olive oil to coat well.

4. In a medium frying pan over medium heat, heat the remaining 2 tablespoons olive oil, add the pancetta and sauté, stirring occasionally until it is just crisp, about 10 minutes. Drain on paper towels. Melt the butter in the pan and add the leeks. Reduce the heat to medium-low and sauté, stirring occasionally until completely wilted and tender, about 20 minutes.

5. In a small bowl, combine the bread crumbs, pecorino romano cheese and salt to taste.

6. To the orzo, add the squash, pancetta and leeks and toss to mix well. Transfer to a 2-qt (2-l) baking dish. Add the Chicken Stock and top with the bread crumb mixture. Bake until the crumbs just begin to color, about 20 minutes.

7. To serve, divide among individual plates. Serve hot.

Serves 6

NUTRITIONAL ANALYSIS: Calories 504 (Kilojoules 2,116); Protein 15 g; Carbohydrates 64 g; Total Fat 21 g; Saturated Fat 8 g; Cholesterol 30 mg; Sodium 683 mg; Dietary Fiber 4 g

FARFALLINE WITH OLIVES AND SUN-DRIED TOMATOES

Because the Preserved Lemons must age for 7 days, you must plan ahead to make this recipe. You can substitute ¼ cup (2 fl oz/60 ml) fresh lemon juice and an additional teaspoon of salt, but the taste will be less complex.

¼ cup (1½ oz/45 g) Preserved Lemons *(recipe on page 125)*

12 sun-dried tomatoes in olive oil, drained

5 qt (5 l) water

1 tablespoon salt

12 oz (375 g) dried farfalline

½ cup (4 fl oz/125 ml) extra-virgin olive oil

¼ cup (2½ oz/75 g) thinly sliced garlic

1 cup (5 oz/155 g) Kalamata or other black olives, pitted

2 tablespoons capers, drained

1 tablespoon grated lemon zest

2 tablespoons minced fresh flat-leaf (Italian) parsley

8 oz (250 g) mozzarella cheese, cut into small pieces

¾ cup (3 oz/90 g) chopped walnuts

1. Make and age the Preserved Lemons.
2. Preheat an oven to 325°F (165°C).
3. In a food mill or blender, purée 9 of the sun-dried tomatoes to make ⅔ cup (5 oz/155 g) of purée. Halve the remaining tomatoes.
4. In a large pot over high heat, bring the water to a boil. Add the salt and the farfalline and cook according to the package directions or until al dente (see page 18), about 6 minutes. Drain well and place in a large bowl.
5. In a small, heavy saucepan over low heat, heat the olive oil. Add the garlic and sauté, stirring frequently, until tender but not brown, about 5 minutes. Cool. Add the Preserved Lemons, tomato purée, Kalamata olives, capers, lemon zest, minced parsley and mozzarella cheese. Add to the pasta. Stir to mix well.
6. Place in a 2-qt (2-l) baking dish and top with the walnuts. Bake until the cheese is completely melted, about 20 minutes.
7. To serve, cool for 5 minutes and divide among individual warmed plates. Garnish with the remaining tomato halves.

Serves 6

NUTRITIONAL ANALYSIS: Calories 829 (Kilojoules 3,481); Protein 19 g; Carbohydrates 61 g; Total Fat 59 g; Saturated Fat 12 g; Cholesterol 29 mg; Sodium 1,059 mg; Dietary Fiber 5 g

Lasagne and Baked Pastas

MACARONI AND CHEESE WITH BACON

Based on the traditional recipe, this rich, cheese-filled comfort food makes a perfect one-dish meal with just a sliced tomato. Tubetti are a common macaroni that are a bit smaller than elbow pasta, which may be substituted.

4 oz (125 g) bacon, cut into strips
  ½ inch (12 mm) wide

6 qt (6 l) water

1 tablespoon salt

1 lb (500 g) dried tubetti

2 cups (16 fl oz/500 ml) milk

1 cup (8 fl oz/250 ml) heavy (double)
  cream

3 eggs, lightly beaten

2 teaspoons mustard powder

  Hot pepper sauce

  Freshly ground pepper

2 cups (8 oz/250 g) grated Fontina
  cheese

2 cups (8 oz/250 g) grated Gruyère
  cheese

2 cups (8 oz/250 g) grated Cheddar
  cheese

2 tablespoons minced fresh flat-leaf
  (Italian) parsley

  Fresh flat-leaf (Italian) parsley
  sprigs

1. Preheat an oven to 375°F (190°C).

2. In a heavy frying pan over medium heat, sauté the bacon until it is just crisp. Drain on paper towels.

3. In a large pot over high heat, bring the water to a boil. Add the salt and tubetti and cook according to the package directions or until almost al dente (see page 18), about 7 minutes. Drain well.

4. In a large bowl, stir together the milk and cream. In a medium bowl, combine the eggs, mustard and hot pepper sauce and pepper to taste. Stir to mix well. Pour the egg mixture into the milk mixture. Add half of the Fontina, Gruyère and Cheddar cheeses and then the tubetti and stir to mix well. Add the remaining half of each cheese and the bacon.

5. Transfer the mixture to a heavy 3-qt (3-l) baking dish. Cover with aluminum foil and bake for 15 minutes. Remove the foil and bake until the center is set, about 15 minutes. Do not overbake.

6. To serve, cool for 5 minutes and divide among individual warmed plates. Sprinkle with an equal amount of minced parsley and garnish with a parsley sprig.

Serves 6

NUTRITIONAL ANALYSIS: Calories 994 (Kilojoules 4,173); Protein 48 g; Carbohydrates 63 g; Total Fat 60 g; Saturated Fat 35 g; Cholesterol 302 mg; Sodium 1,099 mg; Dietary Fiber 2 g

ANGEL HAIR PASTA FLAN

Delicate strands of pasta combine with a rich custard sauce to make a baked pasta of surprising finesse. The goat cheese will cause the surface of the custard to darken more than you might expect before it sets.

4 qt (4 l) water

2 teaspoons salt

8 oz (250 g) dried angel hair pasta

1 red bell pepper (capsicum), roasted, peeled, seeded, deribbed and diced *(see page 121)*

½ cup (2½ oz/75 g) Kalamata olives, pitted and sliced

8 oz (250 g) fresh mild white goat cheese at room temperature

2 cups (16 fl oz/500 ml) milk

8 eggs, lightly beaten

2 cups (16 fl oz/500 ml) heavy (double) cream

1 cup (4 oz/125 g) grated Parmesan cheese

Freshly ground pepper

Fresh flat-leaf (Italian) parsley sprigs

1. Preheat an oven to 325°F (165°C). Butter the inside of a 3-qt (3-l) baking dish.

2. In a large pot over high heat, bring the water to a boil. Add the salt and angel hair pasta and cook according to the package directions or until almost al dente (see page 18), about 4 minutes. Drain well, rinse in cool water, drain again and place in a large bowl. Add the pepper and olives and stir to mix well.

3. In a food processor with the metal blade or a blender, blend the goat cheese and milk until smooth. Transfer to a medium bowl and add the eggs, cream and Parmesan cheese. Stir to mix well.

4. Transfer the pasta to the baking dish and add the cheese and egg mixture. Add the pepper to taste. Bake until the center is set and a knife inserted in the center comes out clean, 40–50 minutes.

5. To serve, cool for 5 minutes and divide among individual warmed plates. Garnish with a parsley sprig.

Serves 6

Nutritional Analysis: Calories 813 (Kilojoules 3,414); Protein 34 g; Carbohydrates 39 g; Total Fat 59 g; Saturated Fat 34 g; Cholesterol 448 mg; Sodium 993 mg; Dietary Fiber 1 g

LEMONY LINGUINE AND CRAB IN PARCHMENT

Using fresh pasta gives these easily assembled parchment parcels a special highlight, but using dried linguine—of any variety—is perfectly acceptable. Slice the fennel bulb very thinly so its taste doesn't overwhelm.

1 lb (500 g) Spinach Pasta *(recipe on page 10)*

6 qt (6 l) water

1 tablespoon salt

2 tablespoons extra-virgin olive oil

1 small fennel bulb, thinly sliced crosswise

3 celery stalks, thinly sliced diagonally

9 oz (280 g) cooked crabmeat

2 tablespoons unsalted butter

2 tablespoons fresh lemon juice
Salt and freshly ground pepper

1 lemon, cut into 6 slices
Fresh fennel fronds

1. Make the Spinach Pasta. Preheat an oven to 375°F (190°C). Cut parchment paper into six 12-x18-inch (30-x45-cm) rectangles.
2. To cut the linguine, roll the pasta sheets into cylinders and cut crosswise into slices ¼ inch (6 mm) wide. Unroll the ribbons and dry 15–30 minutes before cooking.
3. In a large pot over high heat, bring the water to a boil. Add the 1 tablespoon salt and the linguine and cook until tender (see page 18), about 2 minutes. Drain well, rinse in cool water, drain again and place in a medium bowl. Immediately toss with 1 tablespoon of the olive oil.
4. Place the parchment rectangles on a work surface, fold in half crosswise to score and fold open. In the center of one side of each rectangle, place an equal amount of the linguine, fennel, celery, crabmeat, butter, lemon juice and salt and pepper to taste. Top with a lemon slice. To seal the packets closed, brush the outside edge of the parchment with some of the remaining olive oil. Bring the shorter sides together and press to bond the edges. Make a ½-inch (12-mm) hem around each packet to shape semicircles of parchment.
5. Set the packets on a baking sheet and bake until the puffy packets turn golden, about 6 minutes.
6. To serve, using scissors, cut open each package. Garnish with a fennel frond.

Serves 6

NUTRITIONAL ANALYSIS: Calories 347 (Kilojoules 1,459); Protein 18 g; Carbohydrates 43 g; Total Fat 12 g; Saturated Fat 4 g; Cholesterol 124 mg; Sodium 654 mg; Dietary Fiber 3 g

SPAGHETTINI AND SCALLOPS IN PARCHMENT

Baking pasta in parchment makes a beautiful presentation, and the packages can be prepared in advance so that you need only put them in the oven just before serving.

4   tablespoons (2 oz/60 g) Ginger Butter *(recipe on page 123)*

5   qt (5 l) water

1   tablespoon salt

12 oz (375 g) dried spaghettini

2   tablespoons extra-virgin olive oil

18 sea scallops (about 1¼ lb/625 g)

1   green and 3 red bell peppers (capsicums), roasted, peeled, seeded, deribbed and cut into thin strips *(see page 121)*

2   tablespoons fresh lime juice
    Salt and freshly ground pepper

1   lime, cut into 6 slices

1. Make the Ginger Butter. Preheat an oven to 375°F (190°C). Cut parchment paper into six 12-x18-inch (30-x45-cm) rectangles.

2. In a large pot over high heat, bring the water to a boil. Add the 1 tablespoon salt and the spaghettini and cook according to the package directions or until al dente (see page 18), about 8 minutes. Drain well, rinse in cool water, drain again and place in a medium bowl. Immediately toss with 1 tablespoon of the olive oil.

3. In a medium frying pan over medium-low heat, melt 1 tablespoon of the Ginger Butter. Add the scallops in batches and sauté for about 2 minutes on each side.

4. Place the parchment rectangles on a work surface, fold in half crosswise to score and fold open. In the center of one side of each rectangle, place an equal amount of the spaghettini, peppers, scallops, the remaining Ginger Butter, lime juice and salt and pepper to taste. Top with a lime slice. To seal the packets closed, brush the outside edge of the parchment with some of the remaining olive oil. Bring the shorter sides together and press to bond the edges. Make a ½-inch (12-mm) hem around each packet to shape semicircles of parchment.

5. Set the packets on a baking sheet and bake until the puffy packets turn golden, about 8 minutes.

6. To serve, using scissors, cut open each package.

Serves 6

NUTRITIONAL ANALYSIS: Calories 421 (Kilojoules 1,767); Protein 24 g; Carbohydrates 50 g; Total Fat 14 g; Saturated Fat 6 g; Cholesterol 52 mg; Sodium 444 mg; Dietary Fiber 2 g

Lasagne and Baked Pastas

PASTA CARBONARA SOUFFLÉ

Based on the traditional "charcoal-maker's" pasta dish, this recipe produces a rich, golden soufflé encasing delicate pasta strands. A Caesar salad, crusty bread and a platter of olives and roasted peppers are ideal accompaniments.

4 qt (4 l) water

2 teaspoons salt

5 oz (155 g) dried angel hair pasta, broken into thirds

1 tablespoon extra-virgin olive oil

4 oz (125 g) pancetta, diced

1½ cups (12 fl oz/375 ml) half & half (half cream)

7 eggs, separated

¼ cup (⅓ oz/10 g) minced fresh flat-leaf (Italian) parsley

Salt and freshly ground pepper

¾ cup (3 oz/90 g) grated Fontina cheese

½ cup (2 oz/60 g) grated Parmesan cheese

Fresh flat-leaf (Italian) parsley sprigs

1. Preheat an oven to 375°F (190°C). Butter the inside of a 2-qt (2-l) soufflé dish.

2. In a large pot over high heat, bring the water to a boil. Add the 2 teaspoons salt and the angel hair pasta and cook according to the package directions or until al dente (see page 18), about 4 minutes. Drain well, place in a large bowl and immediately toss with the olive oil to coat well.

3. In a small, heavy frying pan over medium-low heat, cook the pancetta until crisp, about 10 minutes. Add the half & half and simmer until it is reduced by one-third, about 10 minutes. Cool to room temperature.

4. In a large bowl, beat the egg yolks until thick. Add the parsley and salt and pepper to taste. Stir the egg mixture into the pancetta mixture. Add the Fontina and Parmesan cheeses. Stir to mix well.

5. In a large bowl, beat the egg whites until soft peaks form. Fold one-third of the egg whites into the egg yolk mixture, then add the pasta, stirring lightly. Carefully fold in the remaining egg whites. Pour the mixture into the soufflé dish. Bake until the top is golden brown, 45–50 minutes.

6. To serve, divide among individual warmed plates. Garnish with a parsley sprig.

Serves 6

NUTRITIONAL ANALYSIS: Calories 438 (Kilojoules 1,841); Protein 22 g; Carbohydrates 22 g; Total Fat 29 g; Saturated Fat 13 g; Cholesterol 306 mg; Sodium 650 mg; Dietary Fiber 1 g

FRITTATA OF CAPELLINI, ONIONS AND PANCETTA

The key to a successful frittata is to remove it from the oven as soon as the eggs have set; any longer and the eggs will release their liquid and lose their delicate texture.

1 cup (3½ oz/105 g) Caramelized Onions *(recipe on page 126)*

4 qt (4 l) water

2 teaspoons salt

8 oz (250 g) dried angel hair pasta

2 tablespoons olive oil

4 oz (125 g) pancetta, finely chopped

8 eggs

1 cup (4 oz/125 g) grated Parmesan cheese

Salt and freshly ground pepper

¼ cup (2 oz/60 g) unsalted butter

1. Make the Caramelized Onions. Preheat an oven to 325°F (165°C).

2. In a large pot over high heat, bring the water to a boil. Add the 2 teaspoons salt and the angel hair pasta and cook according to the package directions or until almost al dente (see page 18), about 4 minutes. Drain well, rinse in cool water, drain again and place in a large bowl. Add the Caramelized Onions and toss to mix well.

3. In a small frying pan over medium heat, heat the olive oil. Add the pancetta and sauté, stirring occasionally, until it is just crisp, about 10 minutes. Cool, add to the pasta and toss to mix well.

4. In a medium bowl, beat the eggs until they are creamy. Add the Parmesan cheese and salt and pepper to taste. Stir to mix well.

5. In a 10-inch (25-cm) ovenproof frying pan over medium-low heat, melt the butter until it foams. Add the pasta mixture and shake the pan so that the pasta is spread evenly. Sauté until the pasta begins to turn golden, 7–8 minutes. Add the egg mixture, reduce the heat to low and cook until the eggs appear slightly firm, about 5 minutes.

6. Place in the oven and bake until the eggs just set, about 10 minutes.

7. To serve, invert onto a large serving plate and divide among individual warmed plates.

Serves 6

NUTRITIONAL ANALYSIS: Calories 559 (Kilojoules 2,347); Protein 24 g; Carbohydrates 37 g; Total Fat 35 g; Saturated Fat 16 g; Cholesterol 339 mg; Sodium 720 mg; Dietary Fiber 2 g

RADIATORI BOLOGNESE WITH ITALIAN MEATBALLS

Think of this as a baked version of spaghetti and meatballs, in which radiatori or other medium shapes replace the slender pasta strands. Note that you'll need to dry bread crumbs for both the meatballs and the crust.

4   cups (32 fl oz/1 l) Bolognese Sauce *(recipe on page 124)*

6   qt (6 l) water

1   tablespoon salt

1   lb (500 g) dried radiatori

4   oz (125 g) mozzarella cheese, cut into small pieces

2   cups (8 oz/250 g) dried bread crumbs *(see page 116)*
     Fresh flat-leaf (Italian) parsley sprigs

ITALIAN MEATBALLS

12 oz (375 g) ground (minced) beef

8   oz (250 g) ground (minced) pork

½   cup (2 oz/60 g) dried bread crumbs *(see page 116)*

½   cup (2 oz/60 g) grated pecorino romano cheese

¼   cup (½ oz/10 g) minced fresh flat-leaf (Italian) parsley

2   garlic cloves, peeled and minced

3   eggs, lightly beaten
     Salt and freshly ground pepper

½   cup (2½ oz/75 g) unbleached all-purpose (plain) flour

2   tablespoons olive oil

1. Preheat an oven to 350°F (180°C). Make the Bolognese Sauce. Prepare the Italian Meatballs (see below).
2. In a large pot over high heat, bring the water to a boil. Add the 1 tablespoon salt and the radiatore and cook according to the package directions or until almost al dente (see page 18), about 7 minutes. Drain well and place in a large bowl. Add two thirds of the Bolognese Sauce. Carefully fold in the Italian Meatballs and mozzarella cheese.
3. Transfer the mixture into a 3-qt (3-l) baking dish. Add the remaining Bolognese Sauce and stir to mix well. Top with the bread crumbs. Bake until hot and bubbly, 25–30 minutes.
4. To serve, cool for 5 minutes and divide among individual warmed plates. Garnish with a parsley sprig.

ITALIAN MEATBALLS

1. In a medium bowl, combine the beef, pork, bread crumbs, pecorino romano cheese, parsley, garlic, eggs and salt and pepper to taste. Stir to mix well.
2. Place the flour in a small bowl. In a small frying pan over medium heat, heat the olive oil. Shape the meat mixture into 40 teaspoon-sized meatballs. Drop each meatball into the bowl of flour and, shaking the bowl, lightly coat each meatball. Fry the meatballs in batches, turning frequently, until uniformly browned, 6–7 minutes. Drain on paper towels.

Serves 8

NUTRITIONAL ANALYSIS: Calories 893 (Kilojoules 3,748); Protein 41 g; Carbohydrates 73 g; Total Fat 47 g; Saturated Fat 17 g; Cholesterol 200 mg; Sodium 1,339 mg; Dietary Fiber 5 g

SAGE-SCENTED SEMOLINA GNOCCHI WITH MOZZARELLA

This typically Roman pasta dumpling, known as gnocchi, uses coarse-ground semolina—not the flour used to make fresh pasta—as the basis for the dough.

8   tablespoons (4 oz/125 g) unsalted butter

2   cups (16 fl oz/500 ml) milk

4   cups (32 fl oz/1 l) water

2   fresh sage sprigs

1⅔ cups (8 oz/250 g) semolina

3   egg yolks

1   cup (4 oz/125 g) grated aged Asiago cheese

1   tablespoon salt

4   oz (125 g) smoked mozzarella cheese, thinly sliced into 48 pieces

48   fresh sage leaves
     Freshly ground pepper

1. Preheat an oven to 425°F (220°C). Coat the sides and bottom of a 13-x17-inch (33-x43-cm) baking sheet with sides and a 9-x13-inch (23-x33-cm) baking dish with 2 tablespoons of the butter.

2. In a medium saucepan over medium heat, bring the milk, water and sage sprigs to a simmer. Remove from the heat and cool for 15 minutes. Remove and discard the sage sprigs. Place the liquid over medium-low heat. Whisk the semolina into the milk. Continue whisking until it thickens, 4–5 minutes. Remove from the heat.

3. In a small bowl, mix the egg yolks with 2 tablespoons of the cooked semolina. Add the egg mixture to the semolina in the saucepan. Quickly stir in the Asiago cheese, 4 tablespoons (2 oz/60 g) of the butter and the salt. Pour onto the baking sheet, using a spatula to spread it evenly. Cool in the refrigerator for at least 30 minutes or up to 1 hour.

4. Using a 2-inch (5-cm) round cookie cutter, cut the semolina into 48 gnocchi. Top each with 1 slice of smoked mozzarella and 1 sage leaf. Place in the baking dish, overlapping them slightly. Cut the remaining 2 tablespoons of butter into small pieces and scatter over the top. Add pepper to taste.

5. Bake for 10 minutes. Increase the heat to 475°F (250°C) and bake until the gnocchi just begin to brown, about 10 minutes longer.

6. To serve, divide among individual warmed plates.

Serves 6

NUTRITIONAL ANALYSIS: Calories 532 (Kilojoules 2,233); Protein 19 g; Carbohydrates 39 g; Total Fat 32 g; Saturated Fat 19 g; Cholesterol 187 mg; Sodium 1,431 mg; Dietary Fiber 2 g

Lasagne and Baked Pastas

PAPPARDELLE WITH SUMMER TOMATO SAUCE

Composed of layers of fresh egg pasta, thinly sliced zucchini (courgettes), ham and a fresh tomato sauce, this delicate baked dish calls for a gentle hand in assembling and serving. Serve with yellow cherry tomatoes.

1¾ cups (14 fl oz/435 ml) Summer Tomato Sauce *(recipe on page 127)*

1½ lb (750 g) Egg Pasta *(recipe on page 11)*

4 small zucchini (courgettes), cut lengthwise into ribbons

8 qt (8 l) water

1½ tablespoons salt

8 oz (250 g) prosciutto, thinly sliced

¾ cup (3 oz/90 g) grated aged Asiago cheese

Fresh flat-leaf (Italian) parsley sprigs

1. Make the Summer Tomato Sauce and Egg Pasta. Preheat an oven to 325°F (165°C).
2. To cut the pappardelle, roll the pasta sheets into cylinders and cut crosswise into slices 1¼ inch (3 cm) wide. Unroll the ribbons and dry 15–30 minutes before cooking.
3. In a medium pot of boiling water, blanch the zucchini ribbons for 1 minute. Drain well.
4. In a large pot over high heat, bring the 8 qt (8 l) water to a boil. Add the 1½ tablespoons salt and the pappardelle and cook until tender (see page 18), about 2 minutes. Drain well and place in a large bowl. Spoon ½ cup (4 fl oz/125 ml) of the Summer Tomato Sauce over the pappardelle and toss to coat well.
5. In a low-sided 3-qt (3-l) gratin dish, layer half the pappardelle, half the zucchini ribbons and half the prosciutto slices. Pour on half of the remaining Summer Tomato Sauce. Add a second layer of the remaining pappardelle, zucchini and prosciutto. Top with the remaining Summer Tomato Sauce and Asiago cheese. Bake until the cheese is completely melted, about 15 minutes.
6. To serve, cool for 5 minutes and divide among individual warmed plates. Garnish with a parsley sprig.

Serves 8

NUTRITIONAL ANALYSIS: Calories 456 (Kilojoules 1,914); Protein 22 g; Carbohydrates 50 g; Total Fat 19 g; Saturated Fat 9 g; Cholesterol 134 mg; Sodium 1,116 mg; Dietary Fiber 5 g

Filled Pastas

STACKED PASTA ROUNDS WITH LAMB AND EGGPLANT

Think of this dish as individual lasagne rounds. If you do not have fresh rosemary, substitute fresh oregano or tarragon. Try the technique with various fillings and sauces for an unusual presentation.

1 lb (500 g) Tomato Pasta *(recipe on page 10)*

6 tablespoons (3 fl oz/80 ml) extra-virgin olive oil

1 large eggplant (aubergine), halved

2 tablespoons minced garlic

1½ lb (750 g) ground (minced) lamb

2 teaspoons minced fresh rosemary

2 lb (1 kg) tomatoes, peeled, seeded and chopped *(see page 122)*

6 qt (6 l) water

1 tablespoon salt

3 red bell peppers (capsicums), roasted, peeled, seeded, deribbed and cut into thin strips *(see page 121)*

1 cup (5 oz/155 g) Kalamata olives, pitted and sliced

8 oz (250 g) fresh mozzarella cheese, thinly sliced

Fresh rosemary sprigs

1. Make the Tomato Pasta and cut it into eighteen 4-inch (10-cm) rounds. Preheat an oven to 375°F (190°C). Line a heavy baking sheet with waxed paper and coat it with 1 tablespoon of the olive oil.

2. Brush the cut surfaces of the eggplant with 1 tablespoon of the olive oil, place them in a baking dish and bake until very soft, about 40 minutes. Cool to the touch. Scoop out the insides and place in a small bowl. Add 2 tablespoons of the olive oil and 1 tablespoon of the garlic and mash well.

3. In a medium frying pan over medium heat, cook the lamb, breaking it up with a fork, until it is no longer pink, about 7 minutes. Add the remaining garlic and the rosemary and remove from the heat. In a small bowl, combine the tomatoes with the remaining olive oil.

4. In a large pot over high heat, bring the water to a boil. Add the 1 tablespoon salt and the pasta rounds and cook until tender (see page 18), about 2 minutes. Drain well.

5. Place 6 pasta rounds on the baking sheet. On each round, layer an equal amount of the eggplant mixture, the lamb mixture, another pasta round and an equal amount of roasted peppers, olives and mozzarella cheese. Top with a third pasta round and an equal amount of the tomato mixture. Bake for 15 minutes.

6. To serve, divide among individual warmed plates. Garnish with a rosemary sprig.

Serves 6

NUTRITIONAL ANALYSIS: Calories 886 (Kilojoules 3,719); Protein 37 g; Carbohydrates 59 g; Total Fat 56 g; Saturated Fat 15 g; Cholesterol 180 mg; Sodium 936 mg; Dietary Fiber 6 g

MANICOTTI WITH GREENS AND SPICY TOMATO SAUCE

Large tubes of dried pasta used for filling are called manicotti. Similar tubes made from fresh pasta rectangles are called cannelloni. The greens mixture can be made from all chard or all spinach, if you prefer.

3 tablespoons unsalted butter

1 small yellow onion, peeled and diced

1 tablespoon minced garlic

1½ lb (750 g) Swiss chard (silverbeet), stemmed and chopped

1 lb (500 g) spinach, stemmed and chopped

4 oz (125 g) mild white goat cheese

1 cup (4 oz/125 g) grated pecorino romano cheese

1 egg, lightly beaten

6 qt (6 l) water

1 tablespoon salt

12 dried manicotti

1 tablespoon chopped flat-leaf (Italian) parsley

SPICY TOMATO SAUCE

3 tablespoons olive oil

1 small yellow onion, peeled and finely diced

1 tablespoon minced garlic

1½ lb (750 g) tomatoes, peeled, seeded and chopped *(see page 122)*

Red pepper flakes

Salt

1. Preheat an oven to 325°F (165°C). Coat the inside of a 9-x13-inch (23-x33-cm) baking dish with olive oil. Prepare the Spicy Tomato Sauce (see below).

2. To make the filling, in a large frying pan over medium-low heat, melt the butter until it foams. Add the onion and sauté, stirring frequently, until tender and fragrant, about 15 minutes. Add the garlic and sauté for 2 minutes. Add the chard and spinach, cover and cook until the greens wilt, about 8 minutes. Cool to room temperature. Add the goat and pecorino romano cheeses and egg. Stir to mix well.

3. In a large pot over high heat, bring the water to a boil. Add the 1 tablespoon salt and the manicotti and cook according to the package directions or until al dente (see page 18), about 12 minutes. Drain well, rinse in cool water and drain again.

4. Fill the manicotti with equal amounts of the filling and place in the baking dish. Top with the Spicy Tomato Sauce. Bake until the sauce is bubbly, about 25 minutes. Garnish with an equal amount of the parsley.

SPICY TOMATO SAUCE

1. In a medium frying pan over medium heat, heat the olive oil. Add the onion and sauté, stirring frequently, until tender and fragrant, about 15 minutes. Add the garlic and sauté for 2 minutes. Reduce the heat to medium-low, add the tomatoes and red pepper flakes and salt to taste and simmer for 15 minutes.

2. Using a food mill or a blender, purée the sauce.

Serves 6

NUTRITIONAL ANALYSIS: Calories 428 (Kilojoules 1,797); Protein 17 g; Carbohydrates 32 g; Total Fat 26 g; Saturated Fat 13 g; Cholesterol 85 mg; Sodium 807 mg; Dietary Fiber 3 g

Filled Pastas

MANICOTTI WITH MUSHROOMS AND GOAT CHEESE SAUCE

Though this recipe calls for a mixture of cremini, button and shiitake mushrooms, feel free to use any combination that you like and can find, or use all button mushrooms.

¼ cup (2 oz/60 g) unsalted butter

2 shallots, peeled and minced

1 tablespoon minced garlic

24 green (spring) onions, green and white parts, cut into small rounds

4 cups (12 oz/360 g) crimini mushrooms

4 cups (12 oz/360 g) button mushrooms

4 cups (12 oz/360 g) shiitake mushrooms, stemmed

6 qt (6 l) water

1 tablespoon salt

12 dried manicotti
    Fresh chives

GOAT CHEESE SAUCE

2 cups (16 fl oz/500 ml) heavy (double) cream

5 oz (155 g) fresh mild white goat cheese, crumbled

1 tablespoon minced fresh chives
    Salt and freshly ground pepper

1. Preheat an oven to 350°F (180°C). Coat the inside of a 9-x13-inch (23-x33-cm) baking dish with olive oil. Prepare the Goat Cheese Sauce (see below).

2. To make the filling, in a large frying pan over medium-low heat, melt the butter until it foams. Add the shallots and sauté until tender, about 5 minutes. Add the garlic and green onions and sauté for 2 minutes. Add the mushrooms, cover and sauté until they are limp, 10–12 minutes. Remove the lid, increase the heat to medium-high and cook until all the liquid has evaporated, 10–15 minutes. Cool to room temperature.

3. In a large pot over high heat, bring the water to a boil. Add the 1 tablespoon salt and the manicotti and cook according to the package directions or until al dente (see page 18), about 12 minutes. Drain well, rinse in cool water and drain again.

4. Fill the manicotti with equal amounts of the filling and place in the baking dish. Top with the Goat Cheese Sauce. Bake until the sauce is bubbly, about 20 minutes.

5. To serve, cool for 5 minutes and divide among individual warmed plates. Garnish with the chives.

GOAT CHEESE SAUCE

1. In a medium saucepan over medium heat, simmer the cream until it is reduced by one-third, about 15 minutes. Remove from the heat, add the goat cheese and stir until the sauce is smooth. Add the chives and salt and pepper to taste.

Serves 6

NUTRITIONAL ANALYSIS: Calories 590 (Kilojoules 2,479); Protein 15 g; Carbohydrates 35 g; Total Fat 46 g; Saturated Fat 28 g; Cholesterol 148 mg; Sodium 256 mg; Dietary Fiber 4 g

CANNELLONI PRIMAVERA WITH PEPPER SAUCE

Primavera, Italian for springtime, aptly describes the mixture of asparagus, zucchini (courgettes) and peas used in the pasta filling; feel free to use other seasonal vegetables, if you like.

1½ cups (12 fl oz/375 ml) Pepper Sauce *(recipe on page 126)*

8 oz (250 g) Lemon Pasta *(recipe on page 10)*

1 cup (5 oz/155 g) fresh shelled peas or frozen peas, thawed

3 tablespoons unsalted butter

1 lb (500 g) asparagus, cut into pieces 2 inches (5 cm) long

2 small zucchini (courgettes), cut into thin strips

2 tablespoons minced fresh mint
Salt and freshly ground pepper

4 qt (4 l) water

2 teaspoons salt
Fresh mint sprigs

1. Make the Pepper Sauce. Make the Lemon Pasta and cut it into twelve 4-x5-inch (10-x13-cm) rectangles. Preheat an oven to 350°F (180°C). Coat the inside of a 9-x13-inch (23-x33-cm) baking dish with olive oil.

2. In a medium saucepan of boiling salted water, cook the peas until tender, about 4 minutes. Drain well.

3. To make the filling, in a medium frying pan over medium-low heat, melt the butter until it foams. Add the asparagus and sauté until tender-crisp, about 8 minutes. Add the zucchini and sauté for 3 minutes. Add the peas, mint and salt and pepper to taste. Cool to room temperature.

4. In a large pot over high heat, bring the water to a boil. Add the 2 teaspoons salt and the pasta rectangles and cook until tender (see page 18), about 2½ minutes. Drain well and set individually on a work surface.

5. Spoon an equal amount of the filling in the center of each pasta rectangle. Roll the short side and place in the baking dish. Top with the Pepper Sauce. Bake until heated through, about 10 minutes.

6. To serve, divide among individual warmed plates. Garnish with a mint sprig.

Serves 6

NUTRITIONAL ANALYSIS: Calories 255 (Kilojoules 1,071); Protein 10 g; Carbohydrates 31 g; Total Fat 11 g; Saturated Fat 5 g; Cholesterol 51 mg; Sodium 331 mg; Dietary Fiber 3 g

$\mathcal{S}$EAFOOD CRESPELLE WITH CHERRY TOMATOES

No cheese or cream is used to bind together this seafood mixture, so take care to handle these crepes as gently as possible to keep the filling from falling out. Vary the seafood mixture according to availability.

12 crespelle *(recipe on page 13)*

8 tablespoons (4 oz/125 g) unsalted butter

12 oz (375 g) medium shrimp (prawns), shelled and deveined *(see page 122)*

8 oz (250 g) bay scallops or sea scallops, halved

1 shallot, peeled and minced

¼ cup (3 oz/90 g) balsamic vinegar

¼ cup (3 oz/90 g) honey, warmed

Salt and freshly ground pepper

18 cherry tomatoes, quartered

¼ cup (¼ oz/7.5 g) thinly sliced fresh mint leaves

Fresh mint sprigs

1. Make the crespelle. Preheat an oven to 325°F (165°C). Coat the inside of a 9-x13-inch (23-x33-cm) baking dish with olive oil.

2. To make the filling, in a medium frying pan over medium-low heat, melt 3 tablespoons of the butter until it foams. Add the shrimp and sauté until they turn pink and curl, about 4 minutes. Using a slotted spoon, remove the shrimp, reserving 12 for garnishing and placing the rest into a medium bowl. To the pan, add another 1 tablespoon of the butter, melt it until it foams, add the scallops and sauté until opaque, about 5 minutes. Transfer to the medium bowl with the shrimp.

3. To the pan, add 2 tablespoons of the butter, melt it until it foams, add the shallot and sauté, stirring frequently, until soft, about 5 minutes. Add the vinegar, honey and salt and pepper to taste. Reduce the heat to low and whisk in the remaining butter.

4. Reserve one-third of the cherry tomatoes. Add the remaining tomatoes, sliced mint and 3 tablespoons of the shallot mixture to the filling. Toss to mix well.

5. Fill the crespelle with equal amounts of the filling, roll and place in the baking dish. Bake until heated through, 7–8 minutes. Heat the remaining shallot mixture.

6. To serve, divide the crespelle among individual warmed plates. Top with an equal amount of the reserved tomatoes and remaining shallot mixture. Garnish with a mint sprig and reserved shrimp.

Serves 6

NUTRITIONAL ANALYSIS: Calories 423 (Kilojoules 1,778); Protein 21 g; Carbohydrates 25 g; Total Fat 27 g; Saturated Fat 12 g; Cholesterol 200 mg; Sodium 313 mg; Dietary Fiber 1 g

CHEESE CRESPELLE WITH SWEET TOMATO SAUCE

A delicate egg-and-goat-cheese mixture fills these oven-baked crepes. The tomato sauce in this recipe complements them with its subtle combination of sweet and spicy seasonings. If you'd prefer, omit the red pepper flakes from the sauce.

12   crespelle *(recipe on page 13)*

1½ cups (12 fl oz/375 ml) Béchamel Sauce *(recipe on page 124)* at room temperature

3   egg yolks, lightly beaten

1   lb (500 g) feta cheese, crumbled

1½ cups (6 oz/185 g) grated Parmesan cheese

¼   cup (⅓ oz/10 g) minced fresh flat-leaf (Italian) parsley

1   tablespoon minced fresh oregano leaves

Freshly ground pepper

Fresh oregano sprigs

SWEET TOMATO SAUCE

2   tablespoons olive oil

1   small yellow onion, peeled and diced

1   lb (500 g) tomatoes, peeled, seeded and chopped *(see page 122)*

1   teaspoon dried oregano

Ground cinnamon

Red pepper flakes

2   teaspoons honey

Salt

1. Make the crespelle and the Béchamel Sauce. Preheat an oven to 375°F (190°C). Coat the inside of a 9-x13-inch (23-x33-cm) baking dish with olive oil. Prepare the Sweet Tomato Sauce (see below).

2. To make the filling, in a medium bowl, combine the Béchamel Sauce and egg yolks. Add the feta and Parmesan cheeses, parsley and oregano and pepper to taste. Stir to mix well.

3. Fill the crespelle with equal amounts of the filling, roll and place in the baking dish. Bake until the filling is completely hot, 12–15 minutes.

4. To serve, divide the Sweet Tomato Sauce among individual warmed plates. Top with 2 crespelle. Garnish with an oregano sprig.

SWEET TOMATO SAUCE

1. In a medium saucepan over medium heat, heat the olive oil. Add the onion and sauté, stirring frequently, until tender and fragrant, about 15 minutes. Add the tomatoes, oregano and cinnamon and red pepper flakes to taste. Simmer for 15 minutes. Add the honey and salt to taste. Stir to mix well. Reheat before serving.

Serves 6

NUTRITIONAL ANALYSIS: Calories 697 (Kilojoules 2,929); Protein 29 g; Carbohydrates 25 g; Total Fat 54 g; Saturated Fat 28 g; Cholesterol 313 mg; Sodium 1,637 mg; Dietary Fiber 1 g

SWEET POTATO CRESPELLE WITH WALNUT SAUCE

Sweet potatoes can be extremely sweet, making this hearty vegetarian main course seem almost like dessert. To cut the sweetness, use half sweet potatoes and half russet potatoes.

12 crespelle *(recipe on page 13)*

3 sweet potatoes (3 lb/1.5 kg)

2 tablespoons unsalted butter, melted

1 cup (4 oz/125 g) grated Parmesan cheese

2 tablespoons chopped walnuts

1 tablespoon minced fresh flat-leaf (Italian) parsley

Salt and freshly ground pepper

Fresh flat-leaf (Italian) parsley sprigs

WALNUT SAUCE

3 tablespoons butter

3 tablespoons chopped walnuts

¾ cup (6 fl oz/180 ml) heavy (double) cream

½ cup (2 oz/60 g) grated Parmesan cheese

1 tablespoon minced fresh flat-leaf (Italian) parsley

Freshly ground pepper

1. Make the crespelle. Preheat an oven to 350°F (180°C). Coat the inside of a 9-x13-inch (23-x33-cm) baking dish with olive oil. Prepare the Walnut Sauce (see below).

2. To make the filling, using a fork, puncture the sweet potatoes in several places and bake until tender, about 45 minutes. Cool to the touch. Cut in half, scoop out the insides, place in a medium bowl and mash. Add the butter, Parmesan cheese, walnuts, minced parsley and salt and pepper to taste. Stir to mix well.

3. Fill the crespelle with equal amounts of the filling, roll and place in the baking dish. Bake until heated through but not brown, about 20 minutes.

4. To serve, divide among individual warmed plates. Top with an equal amount of the Walnut Sauce. Garnish with a parsley sprig.

WALNUT SAUCE

1. In a small saucepan over medium-low heat, melt the butter until it foams. Add the walnuts and sauté for 2 minutes. Add the cream, Parmesan cheese and parsley and pepper to taste. Bring to a simmer. Reheat before serving.

Serves 6

NUTRITIONAL ANALYSIS: Calories 493 (Kilojoules 2,070); Protein 16 g; Carbohydrates 13 g; Total Fat 42 g; Saturated Fat 20 g; Cholesterol 162 mg; Sodium 704 mg; Dietary Fiber 1 g

AGNOLOTTI FLOATING IN MUSHROOM BROTH

Lovers of mushrooms will especially like this delicate, flavorful recipe. For even more complexity, add some diced prosciutto to the mushroom mixture. If time is at a premium, substitute wonton wrappers for the fresh pasta.

1 lb (500 g) Egg Pasta *(recipe on page 10)*

8 oz (250 g) shiitake mushrooms

¼ cup (2 oz/60 g) unsalted butter

1 shallot, peeled and minced

4 tablespoons (⅓ oz/10 g) minced fresh chives

Salt and freshly ground pepper

8 cups (64 fl oz/2 l) Chicken Stock *(recipe on page 125)*

¼ oz (7.5 g) dried porcini mushrooms

2 fresh flat-leaf (Italian) parsley sprigs

2 fresh thyme sprigs

1 teaspoon whole black peppercorns

6 qt (6 l) water

1 tablespoon salt

1. Make the Egg Pasta. Remove and reserve the shiitake mushroom stems. Mince the mushrooms.

2. To make the filling, in a frying pan over medium-low heat, melt the butter until it foams. Add the shallot and sauté until tender, about 10 minutes. Reduce the heat to low, stir in the minced mushrooms, cover and cook until tender and limp, 10–15 minutes. Add 2 tablespoons of the chives and salt and pepper to taste. Stir to mix well.

3. To make the agnolotti, using a 2-inch (5-cm) cookie cutter, cut the pasta into 60 circles. Working with one at a time, using a pastry brush, coat each pasta circle lightly with water. Place about ¾ teaspoon of the filling on one side of each circle. Fold over, lining up the edges and pinch the edges together. Dry 30–60 minutes before cooking.

4. To make the broth, in a large saucepan over medium heat, combine the Chicken Stock, reserved shiitake mushroom stems, dried porcini mushrooms, parsley, thyme and peppercorns and bring to a boil. Reduce the heat to low and simmer, partially covered, for 15 minutes. Remove from the heat and cool for 15 minutes. Strain into a saucepan. Reheat before serving.

5. In a large pot over high heat, bring the water to a boil. Add the 1 tablespoon salt and the agnolotti in batches and cook until they float to the surface, about 2 minutes, and then cook 1 minute more.

6. To serve, ladle an equal amount of the agnolotti and broth into individual soup bowls. Top with the remaining chives.

Serves 6

NUTRITIONAL ANALYSIS: Calories 337 (Kilojoules 1,416); Protein 14 g; Carbohydrates 46 g; Total Fat 13 g; Saturated Fat 6 g; Cholesterol 92 mg; Sodium 620 mg; Dietary Fiber 2 g

LASAGNE PINWHEELS WITH PANCETTA AND LEEK SAUCE

Using the instructions in this recipe, you can use a variety of smooth mixtures, including the sweet potato filling (recipe on page 96) to form pretty pinwheels of many different stripes.

1½ cups (12 fl oz/375 ml) Pancetta and Leek Sauce *(recipe on page 126)*

6 tablespoons (3 fl oz/80 ml) extra-virgin olive oil

1 small yellow onion, peeled and diced

6 garlic cloves, peeled and minced

3 cups (21 oz/655 g) canned cannellini beans, drained

1 cup (4 oz/125 g) freshly grated Parmesan cheese

Salt and freshly ground pepper

6 qt (6 l) water

1 tablespoon salt

18 dried lasagne noodles

6 tablespoons (½ oz/15 g) minced fresh flat-leaf (Italian) parsley

Fresh flat-leaf (Italian) parsley sprigs

1. Make the Pancetta and Leek Sauce. Preheat an oven to 350°F (180°C). Coat the inside of a 9-x13-inch (23-x33-cm) baking dish with olive oil.
2. To make the filling, in a medium frying pan over medium heat, heat 2 tablespoons of the olive oil. Add the onion and sauté, stirring frequently, until tender and fragrant, about 15 minutes. Add the garlic and sauté for 2 minutes. Add the beans and mash into a smooth purée. Add another 3 tablespoons of the olive oil, the Parmesan cheese and salt and pepper to taste. Stir to mix well. Cool to room temperature.
3. In a large pot over high heat, bring the water to a boil. Add the 1 tablespoon salt and the lasagne noodles and cook according to the package directions or until al dente (see page 18), about 12 minutes. Drain well, rinse in cool water and drain again. Spread them out on a work surface.
4. Spread an equal amount of the filling over each noodle and sprinkle with 1 teaspoon of the parsley. Roll each noodle lengthwise, then cut in half. Set them, cut side down, in the baking dish. Using a pastry brush, coat the top and outside of each with some of the remaining 1 tablespoon olive oil. Bake until heated through, about 15 minutes.
5. To serve, divide an equal amount of the Pancetta and Leek Sauce among individual warmed plates. Top with 6 lasagne pinwheels. Garnish with a parsley sprig.

Serves 6

NUTRITIONAL ANALYSIS: Calories 697 (Kilojoules 2,928); Protein 26 g; Carbohydrates 77 g; Total Fat 33 g; Saturated Fat 8 g; Cholesterol 24 mg; Sodium 916 mg; Dietary Fiber 7 g

BEET FAZZOLETTI WITH ORANGE VINAIGRETTE

Bright colors, tastes and fragrances give this sweet-and-sour dish a winning character. An ideal accompaniment to the pasta is beet greens, quickly sautéed with a little garlic and splashed with a bit of the orange vinaigrette.

1 lb (500 g) Beet Pasta *(recipe on page 10)*

¾ lb (12 oz/375 g) beets, about 3 beets

2 tablespoons chopped walnuts, toasted *(see page 120)*

1 tablespoon minced orange zest

½ teaspoon minced fresh tarragon
Salt and freshly ground pepper

6 qt (6 l) water

1 tablespoon salt
Fresh tarragon sprigs

ORANGE VINAIGRETTE

⅓ cup (3 fl oz/80 ml) fresh orange juice

1 tablespoon white wine vinegar

1 small shallot, peeled and minced

½ teaspoon minced fresh tarragon

½ cup (4 fl oz/125 ml) walnut oil

1 tablespoon chopped walnuts, toasted *(see page 120)*
Salt and freshly ground pepper

1. Make the Beet Pasta and cut it into twenty-four 4-inch (10-cm) squares called fazzoletti. Let dry 15–30 minutes before cooking. Preheat an oven to 375°F (190°C). Prepare the Orange Vinaigrette (see below).

2. To make the filling, place the beets in a small ovenproof dish and bake until tender, 30–50 minutes, depending on the size of the beets. Cool to the touch. Peel, finely chop and place in a small bowl. Add the walnuts, orange zest, tarragon and salt and pepper to taste. Toss to mix well.

3. In a large pot over high heat, bring the water to a boil. Add the 1 tablespoon salt and the fazzoletti and cook until tender (see page 18), about 2 minutes. Drain well and spread them out on a work surface.

4. Place about 2 tablespoons of the filling in the center of each fazzoletto, fold in half diagonally and then bring the bottom corners together to form a small triangle.

5. To serve, divide among individual warmed plates. Top with an equal amount of the Orange Vinaigrette. Garnish with a tarragon sprig.

ORANGE VINAIGRETTE

1. In a small saucepan over medium heat, simmer the orange juice, vinegar, shallot and tarragon until the liquid is reduced to ¼ cup (2 fl oz/60 ml), about 5 minutes. Remove from the heat and add the walnut oil and walnuts and salt and pepper to taste. Reheat before serving.

Serves 6

NUTRITIONAL ANALYSIS: Calories 435 (Kilojoules 1,827); Protein 10 g; Carbohydrates 48 g; Total Fat 23 g; Saturated Fat 2 g; Cholesterol 71 mg; Sodium 508 mg; Dietary Fiber 3 g

$\mathcal{S}$WISS CHARD FAZZOLETTI WITH SHALLOT VINAIGRETTE

The fresh pasta in this simple, delicate dish is filled and folded after cooking. If you like, use Egg Pasta instead of the black pepper variation. The light vinaigrette dressing makes the dish ideal for a lunch or a summer supper.

1 lb (500 g) Black Pepper Pasta
  (recipe on page 10)

3 tablespoons olive oil

1 shallot, peeled and minced

2 lb (1 kg) Swiss chard (silverbeet),
  leaves and stems chopped
  separately

5 garlic cloves, peeled and minced

6 qt (6 l) water

1 tablespoon salt
  Fresh flat-leaf (Italian) parsley
  sprigs

SHALLOT VINAIGRETTE

3 tablespoons Clarified Butter
  (recipe on page 123)

2 tablespoons finely chopped
  pancetta

3 shallots, peeled and minced

⅓ cup (3 fl oz/80 ml) white wine
  vinegar

1 tablespoon minced fresh flat-leaf
  (Italian) parsley
  Salt and freshly ground pepper

½ cup (4 fl oz/125 ml) extra-virgin
  olive oil

1. Make the Black Pepper Pasta and cut it into twenty-four 4-inch (10-cm) squares called fazzoletti. Let dry 15–30 minutes before cooking. Prepare the Shallot Vinaigrette (see below).

2. To make the filling, in a medium frying pan over medium heat, heat the olive oil. Add the shallot and chopped chard stems and sauté until tender, 5 minutes. Add the garlic and sauté for 2 minutes. Add the chopped chard leaves and cook, stirring frequently, until they wilt, about 8 minutes. Remove from the heat.

3. In a large pot over high heat, bring the water to a boil. Add the 1 tablespoon salt and the fazzoletti and cook until tender (see page 18), about 2 minutes. Drain well and spread them out on a work surface.

4. Place about 2 tablespoons of the filling in the center of each fazzoletto, fold in half diagonally and then bring the bottom corners together to form a small triangle.

5. To serve, divide among individual warmed plates. Top with an equal amount of the Shallot Vinaigrette. Garnish with a parsley sprig.

SHALLOT VINAIGRETTE

1. In a small saucepan over medium-low heat, heat the Clarified Butter. Add the pancetta and sauté until it is just crisp, about 8 minutes. Add the shallots and sauté until tender, 5 minutes. Add the vinegar, parsley and salt and pepper to taste and simmer for 1 minute. Add the olive oil and immediately remove from the heat. Reheat before serving.

Serves 6

NUTRITIONAL ANALYSIS: Calories 538 (Kilojoules 2,259); Protein 12 g; Carbohydrates 47 g; Total Fat 35 g; Saturated Fat 8 g; Cholesterol 89 mg; Sodium 699 mg; Dietary Fiber 2 g

Ravioli and Lasagne

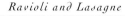

ICOTTA FILLED SHELLS WITH BOLOGNESE SAUCE

A blend of ricotta and spinach is one of the classic fillings for baked shells. For a vegetarian version of the dish, omit the prosciutto and use Spicy Tomato Sauce (see page 87) in place of the Bolognese Sauce.

4   cups (32 fl oz/1 l) Bolognese Sauce *(recipe on page 124)*

3   tablespoons butter

1   shallot, peeled and minced

6   garlic cloves, peeled and minced

1   lb (500 g) spinach, stemmed and coarsely chopped

1   cup (8 oz/250 g) whole-milk ricotta cheese

4   oz (125 g) prosciutto, diced

¾   cup (3 oz/90 g) plus 2 tablespoons grated Parmesan cheese

    Salt and freshly ground pepper

6   qt (6 l) water

1   tablespoon salt

18   dried jumbo pasta shells

1. Make the Bolognese Sauce. Preheat an oven to 325°F (165°C).

2. To make the filling, in a large frying pan over medium-low heat, melt the butter until it foams. Add the shallot and sauté, stirring frequently, until soft, about 5 minutes. Add the garlic and sauté for 2 minutes. Add the spinach and cook, stirring frequently, until it is wilted, about 8 minutes. Cool to room temperature. Add the ricotta cheese, prosciutto, the ¾ cup (3 oz/90 g) Parmesan cheese and salt and pepper to taste. Stir to mix well.

3. In a large pot over high heat, bring the water to a boil. Add the 1 tablespoon salt and the shells and cook according to the package directions or until almost al dente (see page 18), about 8 minutes. Drain well, rinse in cool water and drain again.

4. Fill each pasta shell with about 2 tablespoons of the filling and place in a 9-x13-inch (23-x33-cm) baking dish. Top with half of the Bolognese Sauce. Bake until heated through but not brown, about 15 minutes. Heat the remaining Bolognese Sauce.

5. To serve, divide the remaining Bolognese Sauce among individual warmed plates. Top with an equal number of shells and the 2 tablespoons Parmesan cheese.

Serves 6

Nutritional Analysis: Calories 683 (Kilojoules 2,870); Protein 37 g; Carbohydrates 42 g; Total Fat 41 g; Saturated Fat 18 g; Cholesterol 120 mg; Sodium 1,773 mg; Dietary Fiber 5 g

Filled Pastas

CAPONATA FILLED SHELLS
WITH BÉCHAMEL SAUCE

Caponata, Italy's answer to the ratatouille of southern France, has a tangy flavor due to the addition of olives, capers and vinegar. This dish may be assembled well ahead of time and refrigerated.

3   cups (24 fl oz/750 ml) Béchamel Sauce *(recipe on page 124)*

¼   cup (2 fl oz/60 ml) extra-virgin olive oil

1   yellow onion, peeled and finely diced

2   tablespoons minced garlic

1   large eggplant (aubergine), peeled and cubed

2   tomatoes, peeled, seeded and diced *(see page 122)*

½   cup (2½ oz/75 g) black olives, pitted and halved

½   cup (2½ oz/75 g) green olives, pitted and halved

2   tablespoons capers, drained

1   tablespoon red wine vinegar

¼   cup (⅓ oz/10 g) minced fresh flat-leaf (Italian) parsley
    Salt and freshly ground pepper

6   qt (6 l) water

1   tablespoon salt

18 dried jumbo pasta shells
    Fresh flat-leaf (Italian) parsley leaves

1. Make the Béchamel Sauce. Preheat an oven to 350°F (180°C). Coat the inside of a 9-x13-inch (23-x33-cm) baking dish with olive oil.

2. To make the filling, in a large frying pan over low heat, heat the olive oil. Add the onion and sauté, stirring frequently, until tender and fragrant, about 15 minutes. Add the garlic and sauté for 2 minutes. Add the eggplant and sauté until the eggplant is very soft, about 20 minutes. Add the tomatoes, olives, capers, vinegar and minced parsley and simmer for 15 minutes. Add salt and pepper to taste.

3. In a large pot over high heat, bring the water to a boil. Add the 1 tablespoon salt and the shells and cook according to the package directions or until almost al dente (see page 18), about 8 minutes. Drain well, rinse in cool water and drain again.

4. Fill each pasta shell with about 2 tablespoons of filling and place in the baking dish. Top with half of the Béchamel Sauce. Bake until heated through but not brown, about 15 minutes. Heat the remaining Béchamel Sauce.

5. Divide the remaining Béchamel Sauce among individual warmed plates. Top with an equal number of shells. Garnish with a few parsley leaves.

Serves 6

NUTRITIONAL ANALYSIS: Calories 561 (Kilojoules 2,354); Protein 11 g; Carbohydrates 46 g; Total Fat 39 g; Saturated Fat 17 g; Cholesterol 86 mg; Sodium 871 mg; Dietary Fiber 4 g

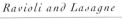

SPINACH PASTA ROLLS WITH SUMMER TOMATO SAUCE

The spiral-patterned green-and-white slices of this pasta roll make a festive presentation with a bright red tomato sauce. The roll can be filled several hours in advance. Have cheesecloth (muslin) and cotton string on hand to form the rolls.

1   lb (500 g) Spinach Pasta *(recipe on page 10)*, rolled by hand into two rectangles 10 x 14 inches (25 x 35 cm)

1¾ cups (14 fl oz/435 ml) Summer Tomato Sauce *(recipe on page 127)*

3   tablespoons olive oil

1   tablespoon minced garlic

2   lb (1 kg) spinach, stemmed and chopped

2   eggs, lightly beaten

½   cup (2 oz/ 60 g) chopped walnuts, toasted *(see page 120)*

1   cup (4 oz/125 g) grated Parmesan cheese

2   cups (1 lb/500 g) whole-milk ricotta cheese
    Salt and freshly ground pepper

6   qt (6 l) water

1   tablespoon salt
    Fresh flat-leaf (Italian) parsley sprigs

1. Make the Spinach Pasta and Summer Tomato Sauce.
2. To make the filling, in a large frying pan over medium heat, heat the olive oil. Add the garlic and sauté until tender, 2 minutes. Add the spinach, reduce the heat to medium-low, cover and cook until it wilts, about 4 minutes. Remove the lid, increase the heat and simmer until all of the liquid has evaporated, about 4 minutes. Cool to room temperature. Place the spinach in a medium bowl. Add the eggs, walnuts, Parmesan and ricotta cheeses and salt and pepper to taste. Stir to mix well.
3. Place the pasta on a floured work surface. Using a rubber spatula, spread half of the filling evenly over one sheet of the pasta, leaving a 1-inch (2.5-cm) margin on all sides. Roll the pasta tightly lengthwise. Wrap with two thicknesses of cheesecloth (muslin). Tie the ends securely with cotton string. Repeat with the second sheet of pasta.
4. In a large wide pot over high heat, bring the water to a boil. Add the 1 tablespoon salt and carefully place the pasta rolls in the water and cook for 20 minutes. Remove from the water and cool for 5 minutes. Using a sharp knife, cut and remove the cheesecloth. Slice each roll.
5. To serve, divide the pieces among individual warmed plates. Top with an equal amount of Summer Tomato Sauce. Garnish with a parsley sprig.

Serves 6

NUTRITIONAL ANALYSIS: Calories 747 (Kilojoules 3,138); Protein 33 g; Carbohydrates 60 g; Total Fat 44 g; Saturated Fat 19 g; Cholesterol 224 mg; Sodium 963 mg; Dietary Fiber 8 g

Filled Pastas

$\mathcal{L}$AMB FILLED SHELLS WITH TOMATO AND LEMON SAUCE

You can make these shells several hours in advance and bake them just before serving. The amount of sauce is just enough to add a contrasting flavor but not enough to overwhelm the other ingredients.

1¼ lb (625 g) ground (minced) lamb

3 garlic cloves, peeled and minced

8 oz (250 g) spinach, stemmed and coarsely chopped

2 teaspoons grated lemon zest

3½ oz (105 g) feta cheese, cut into ¼-inch (6-mm) cubes

6 qt (6 l) water

1 tablespoon salt

18 dried jumbo pasta shells

3 tablespoons pine nuts, toasted (*see page 120*)

1 lemon, cut into 6 slices

TOMATO AND LEMON SAUCE

1 cup (8 fl oz/250 ml) canned tomato sauce

½ cup (4 fl oz/125 ml) Chicken Stock (*recipe on page 125*)

3 tablespoons fresh lemon juice

Salt and freshly ground pepper

1. Preheat an oven to 325°F (165°C). Prepare the Tomato and Lemon Sauce (see below).

2. To make the filling, in a large frying pan over medium heat, cook the ground lamb, breaking it up with a fork, until it is no longer pink. Drain off any excess fat and return the frying pan to the heat. Add the garlic and spinach, cover and cook until the spinach is wilted, 3–4 minutes. Cool to room temperature. Add the lemon zest and feta cheese and toss to mix well.

3. In a large pot over high heat, bring the water to a boil. Add the 1 tablespoon salt and the shells and cook according to the package directions or until almost al dente (see page 18), about 8 minutes. Drain well, rinse in cool water and drain again.

4. Fill each pasta shell with about 2 tablespoons of filling and place in a 9-x13-inch (23-x33-cm) baking dish. Top with half of the Tomato and Lemon Sauce and all of the pine nuts. Bake until heated through but not brown, about 15 minutes. Heat the remaining Tomato and Lemon Sauce.

5. To serve, divide among individual warmed plates. Top with an equal amount of the remaining Tomato and Lemon Sauce. Garnish with a lemon slice.

TOMATO AND LEMON SAUCE

1. In a small, heavy saucepan over medium-low heat, combine the tomato sauce, Chicken Stock, lemon juice and salt and pepper to taste and bring to a boil. Remove from the heat. Stir to mix well.

Serves 6

NUTRITIONAL ANALYSIS: Calories 402 (Kilojoules 1,688); Protein 26 g; Carbohydrates 33 g; Total Fat 20 g; Saturated Fat 8 g; Cholesterol 78 mg; Sodium 631 mg; Dietary Fiber 3 g

$\mathcal{S}$PINACH TORTELLINI WITH GORGONZOLA CREAM SAUCE

Rich, tangy Gorgonzola cheese flavors both the filling and the sauce in this memorable recipe. Tortellini must be made from fresh pasta, but you can prepare them up to 2 days in advance and refrigerate.

1 lb (500 g) Spinach Pasta *(recipe on page 10)*

4 oz (125 g) fresh mild white goat cheese, crumbled

3 oz (90 g) Gorgonzola cheese at room temperature

¾ cup (3 oz/90 g) grated pecorino romano cheese

3 oz (90 g) thinly sliced prosciutto, minced

1 egg, lightly beaten

1 teaspoon minced fresh flat-leaf (Italian) parsley

1 teaspoon minced fresh chives

½ teaspoon freshly ground pepper

6 qt (6 l) water

1 tablespoon salt

Fresh chives

GORGONZOLA CREAM SAUCE

1 cup (8 fl oz/250 ml) heavy (double) cream

6 oz (185 g) Italian Gorgonzola cheese, cut into pieces

1 tablespoon minced fresh chives

Freshly ground pepper

1. Make the Spinach Pasta. Prepare the Gorgonzola Cream Sauce (see below).

2. To make the filling, in a bowl, blend the cheeses, prosciutto, egg, parsley, minced chives and pepper.

3. Using a 2-inch (5-cm) cookie cutter, cut the pasta into 72 circles. Working with one at a time, using a pastry brush, coat each circle lightly with water. Place about ¾ teaspoon of the filling in the center. Fold over, lining up the edges; pinch the edges together. Pull the ends together, wrapping the pasta around the tip of your finger and pinching the ends together. Let dry for 30–60 minutes before cooking.

4. In a large pot over high heat, bring the water to a boil. Add the 1 tablespoon salt and the tortellini in batches and cook until they float to the top, about 3 minutes, and cook for 1 minute more. Spoon a small amount of the Gorgonzola Cream Sauce into a large bowl. Using a slotted spoon, transfer the tortellini to the bowl with the sauce and toss to coat.

5. To serve, divide among individual warmed plates. Top with an equal amount of the remaining Gorgonzola Cream Sauce. Garnish with the chives.

GORGONZOLA CREAM SAUCE

1. In a medium saucepan over medium heat, bring the cream to a simmer. Reduce the heat to medium-low, add the Gorgonzola cheese and stir until the cheese melts. Remove from the heat. Add the chives and pepper to taste. Reheat before serving.

Serves 6

NUTRITIONAL ANALYSIS: Calories 670 (Kilojoules 2,813); Protein 30 g; Carbohydrates 41 g; Total Fat 43 g; Saturated Fat 26 g; Cholesterol 239 mg; Sodium 1,691 mg; Dietary Fiber 2 g

Filled Pastas

Basic Terms and Techniques

The following entries provide a reference source for this volume, offering definitions of essential or unusual ingredients and explanations of fundamental techniques as they relate to the preparation of ravioli, lasagne and other baked and filled pasta dishes.

ANCHOVY FILLETS

These tiny saltwater fish, relatives of sardines, are most commonly found as canned fillets that have been salted and preserved in oil. Imported anchovy fillets packed in olive oil are the most commonly available.

BEANS

All manner of dried beans and lentils may be combined with pasta in baked and filled dishes. Among these, one of the most popular is Italy's cannellini, a variety of white, thin-skinned oval beans, for which Great Northern or white (navy) beans may be substituted.

To Sort and Soak Dried Beans: Before use, dried beans should be carefully picked over to remove any that are discolored or misshapen, or any foreign objects such as small stones or fibers. Soak them in cold water to cover for 3 hours or overnight to shorten their cooking time and improve their digestibility.

BEET GREENS

The slightly bitter leaves of beets have long been enjoyed as a cooked vegetable in their own right. If beet greens are unavailable, spinach or Swiss chard (silverbeet), both related vegetables, may be substituted. Wash all greens thoroughly before adding to recipes.

BREAD CRUMBS

Among their many culinary uses, bread crumbs may be used to add body to pasta fillings or to form a crunchy, golden topping on baked dishes. The crumbs are easily made at home, though dried crumbs may also be found packaged in food stores.

To Make Dried Bread Crumbs: Start with a good-quality rustic-style loaf made of unbleached wheat flour, with a firm, coarse-textured crumb. Cut away the crusts and crumble the bread by hand or in a blender or a food processor with the metal blade. To dry the crumbs, spread them on a baking sheet and dry slowly, about 1 hour, in an oven set at its lowest temperature. Store in a tightly covered container in a cool, dark place.

BUTTER

For the recipes in this book, unsalted butter is preferred. Lacking salt, it allows the cook greater leeway in seasoning recipes to taste and meeting the dietary needs of diners.

CAPERS

The small, pickled flower buds of a bush native to Asia and common to Mediterranean countries, capers are used whole as a savory flavoring or garnish to add spark to rice dishes.

CHEESES

Whether used as part of a filling, as a topping or in a sauce, many different kinds of cheese contribute to the character of baked and filled pastas. Store all cheeses in tightly covered containers in a low-humidity section of a refrigerator. Most cheeses will keep for several months.

ASIAGO Originating in the Italian village of the same name, this firm-textured, piquant cow's-milk cheese may be eaten fresh or aged for up to 6 months, at which time it is often used in grated form.

CHEDDAR A firm, smooth whole-milk cheese, pale yellow-white to deep yellow-orange in color. Cheddar ranges in taste from mild and sweet when fresh to rich and tangy when aged.

FETA The crumbly Greek-style cheese is made from goat's or sheep's milk, notable for its salty sharp flavor.

FONTINA A firm, creamy, mild-tasting Italian sheep's-milk cheese.

GOAT CHEESE Most cheeses made from goat's milk are fresh and creamy, with a distinctive sharp tang; they are sold shaped into small rounds or logs. Some are coated with pepper, ash or a mixture of herbs, which mildly flavors them. Also known as *chèvre*.

GORGONZOLA A creamy, blue-veined Italian cheese. Other creamy blue cheeses may be substituted.

GRUYÈRE A variety of Swiss cheese, Gruyère has a firm, smooth texture, small holes and a strong, nutty flavor.

MOZZARELLA A rindless white, mild-tasting Italian cheese traditionally made from water buffalo's milk and sold fresh. Commercially produced and packaged cow's-milk mozzarella is now more common, although it has less flavor. Look for fresh mozzarella, which is sold immersed in water. When a recipe calls for whole-milk mozzarella, study the label carefully; some brands may be made at least partly with skim milk. Mozzarella is also sometimes smoked, yielding a firmer textured, aromatic but still mild cheese.

PARMESAN A semi-hard cheese made from half skim and half whole cow's milk, with a sharp, salty flavor that results from up to 2 years of aging. In its prime, a good piece of Parmesan cheese is dry but not grainy and flakes easily. For best flavor, buy Parmesan in block form and grate or shave it just before use.

PECORINO ROMANO An Italian sheep's milk cheese, sold either fresh or aged.

RICOTTA A very light and bland Italian cheese traditionally made from twice-cooked sheep's milk, although cow's-milk ricotta is far more common.

To Grate Cheese: In most cases, firm to hard-textured cheeses should be grated with the firm rasps of a cheese grater or cut into thin shreds with the small holes of a shredder: the finer the particles of cheese, the more readily they will melt. Thin shavings of cheese, cut with a cheese shaver or a swivel-bladed vegetable peeler, make an attractive and flavorful garnish.

CITRUS FRUITS

The lively flavor of citrus fruits, in the form of juice or zest, adds fresh spark to many baked and filled pastas.

TO ZEST A CITRUS FRUIT

1. Using a zester, or fine shredder, draw its thin, sharp-edged holes along the surface of the fruit to remove the zest in fine shreds.

2. Alternatively, using a vegetable peeler or a paring knife, remove the zest, then cut it into thin strips.

3. For finely grated zest, use a fine hand-held grater. Vigorously rub the fruit against the sharp teeth.

CRABMEAT

Cooked crabmeat may be found in fish markets or the seafood counters of quality food markets. Frequently, it has been frozen; for the best flavor and texture, seek out freshly cooked crabmeat. In season, from September to April, fish markets will usually sell crabs boiled or steamed whole; ask for them to be cracked, so that you can open the shells by hand and remove the meat. Left in coarse chunks, the shelled meat, especially from the body, is sold as "lump"crabmeat; finer particles from the legs or broken down from larger lumps is known as "flaked" crabmeat.

EGGS

Eggs are sold in the United States in a range of standard sizes, the most common being jumbo, extra large, large and medium. The recipes in this book, including those for making fresh pasta, were created using large Grade A eggs.

To Separate an Egg: Crack the shell in half by tapping it against the side of a bowl, then breaking it apart with your fingers. Holding the shell halves over the bowl, gently transfer the whole yolk back and forth between them, letting the clear white drop away into the bowl and taking care not to cut into the yolk with the edges of the shell. Transfer the yolk to another bowl.

Alternatively, gently pour the egg from the shell onto the slightly cupped fingers of your outstretched clean hand, held over a bowl. Let the whites fall between your fingers into the bowl; the whole yolk will remain in your hand.

The same basic function can be performed by an aluminum, ceramic or plastic egg separator placed over a bowl. The separator holds the yolk intact in its cuplike center while allowing the white to drip out through one or more slots in its side into the bowl.

Store separated eggs in tightly covered containers in the refrigerator for up to 4 days.

1. To peel, place the clove on a work surface and cover it with the side of a large knife. Press down to crush the clove slightly; slip off the dry skin.

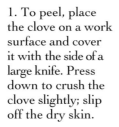

2. To mince, use a sharp knife to cut the peeled clove into thin slices. Then cut across the slices to make thin strips.

3. Using a gentle rocking motion, cut back and forth across the strips to mince them into fine particles.

4. Alternatively, press the peeled clove through a garlic press.

GARLIC

Popular worldwide as a flavoring ingredient, whether raw or cooked, this pungent bulb is best purchased in whole heads composed of individual cloves, to be separated from the head as needed. It is best not to purchase more than you will use in 1–2 weeks, as garlic can shrivel and lose its flavor with prolonged storage.

GINGER

The rhizome of the tropical ginger plant, strong-flavored ginger is a popular savory and sweet spice. Whole ginger rhizomes, commonly but mistakenly called roots, can be purchased fresh in a food store or vegetable market. Candied or crystallized ginger, made by preserving pieces of ginger in sugar syrup and then coating them with granulated sugar, is available in specialty-food shops or in the baking or Asian food sections of well-stocked stores.

To Prepare Fresh Ginger: Before slicing, chopping or grating, the rhizome's brown, papery skin is usually peeled away from the amount being used. The ginger may then be sliced or chopped with a small paring knife or a chef's knife, or grated against the fine holes of a small grater.

HERBS

Many fresh and dried herbs may be used to enhance the flavor of baked and filled pastas. In general, add fresh herbs toward the end of cooking, as their flavor dissipates with long exposure to heat; use dried herbs in dishes that cook longer; they are more concentrated in flavor than their fresh counterparts. Store fresh herbs in water—as you would cut flowers—awaiting use.

HOT PEPPER SAUCE

This bottled commercial cooking and table sauce is made from fresh or dried hot red chilies. Many varieties are available, but Tabasco is the most commonly known brand.

LEEKS

Grown in sandy soil, these leafy-topped, multilayered vegetables require thorough cleaning.

To Clean a Leek: Trim off the tough ends of the dark green leaves. Trim off the roots. If a recipe calls for leek whites only, trim off the dark green leaves where they meet the slender pale green part of the stem. Starting about 1 inch (2.5 cm) from the root end, slit the leek lengthwise. Vigorously swish the leek in a basin or sink filled with cold water. Drain and rinse again; check to make sure that no dirt remains between the tightly packed pale portion of the leaves.

MUSHROOMS

With their meaty textures and rich, earthy flavors, mushrooms enrich many baked and filled pasta dishes. Cultivated white and brown mushrooms are widely available in food markets and green grocers; in their smallest form, with their caps still closed, they are often descriptively called button mushrooms. Cremini mushrooms are similar in size and shape to cultivated mushrooms, but their flavor is richer and their skin has a rich brown color. Shiitake mushrooms, a meaty-flavored Asian variety,

have flat, dark brown caps usually 2–3 inches (5–7.5 cm) in diameter and are available fresh with increasing frequency, particularly in Asian food shops; they are also sold dried. Porcini, the widely used Italian name for rich, meaty-flavored wild mushrooms (also known by the French name cèpes) are commonly sold in dried form.

To Reconstitute Dried Mushrooms: Put the mushrooms in a large bowl and add water to cover. Leave them until soft, about 20 minutes. Lift them from the water, rinse briefly and trim off any tough stems. If you wish to use the soaking liquid as a flavoring, strain it through a double layer of cheesecloth (muslin) to remove any grit or other impurities.

NUTS

Many varieties of nuts may be used to add rich flavor and crunchy texture to baked and filled pastas.

To Toast Nuts: Toasting brings out the full flavor and aroma of nuts. To toast any kind of nut, preheat an oven to 325°F (165°C). Spread the nuts in a single layer on a baking sheet and toast in the oven until they just begin to change color, 5-10 minutes. Remove from the oven and let cool to room temperature. Alternatively, toast nuts in a dry heavy frying pan over low heat, stirring frequently to prevent scorching.

OLIVE OIL

With its rich flavor, its palette of colors from deep green to pale golden and its range of culinary uses, olive oil deserves its reputation as the queen of edible oils. Extra-virgin olive oil is the finest, with a fruity taste and a low acidity that makes it smooth on the palate when used in uncooked dishes or added to hot dishes at the end of cooking. Both virgin and pure olive oils have slightly higher acidity levels and are fine as cooking mediums and for preparing baking dishes to prevent sticking.

PANCETTA

Cured simply with salt and pepper, this Italian-style unsmoked bacon may be sold flat or rolled into a large sausage shape. It is most often used finely chopped as a flavoring ingredient. Sold in Italian delicatessens and specialty-food stores.

PEPPERS

Fresh, sweet-fleshed bell peppers (capsicums) are most common in the unripe green form, although ripened red or yellow varieties are also available. Creamy pale yellow, orange and purple-black types may also be found.

To Prepare a Bell Pepper: Cut the pepper in half lengthwise with a sharp knife. Pull out the stem section from each half, along with the cluster of seeds attached to it. Remove any remaining seeds, along with any thin white membranes, or ribs, to which they are attached. Cut the pepper halves into quarters, strips or thin slices, as called for in the specific recipe.

PROSCIUTTO

A specialty of Parma, Italy, this variety of raw ham is cured by dry-salting for 1 month, followed by air-drying in cool curing sheds for half a year or more. It is usually cut into tissue-thin slices, the better to appreciate its intense flavor and deep pink color.

TO ROAST AND PEEL PEPPERS

1. Preheat a broiler (griller). Cut the bell peppers in half lengthwise and remove the stems, seeds and ribs as directed above.

2. Place the pepper halves on a broiler pan, cut-side down, and broil (grill) until the skins are evenly blackened.

3. Transfer the peppers to a paper bag, close it and let stand until the peppers soften and are cool to the touch, about 10 minutes.

4. Using your fingertips or a small knife, peel off the blackened skins. Then tear or cut the peppers as directed in the recipe.

SHALLOTS

These small members of the onion family have brown skins, white-to-purple flesh and taste like a cross between sweet onion and garlic, making them a versatile seasoning in pasta dishes.

SHRIMP

Fresh, raw shrimp (prawns) are generally sold with the heads already removed but the shells still intact. Before or after their initial cooking, they are usually peeled and their thin, veinlike intestinal tracts removed.

To Peel and Devein Shrimp: Using your thumbs, split open the thin shell along the inner curve, between the two rows of legs. Peel away the shell, taking care—if the recipe calls for it—to leave the last segment with tail fin intact and attached to the meat. Using a small, sharp knife, carefully make a shallow slit along the back, just deep enough to expose the long, usually dark, veinlike intestinal tract. With the tip of the knife or your fingers, lift up and pull out the vein and discard it.

TOMATOES

During summer, when tomatoes are in season, use the best red or yellow sun-ripened tomatoes you can find. At other times of year, plum tomatoes, sometimes called Roma or egg tomatoes, are likely to have the best flavor and texture; for cooking, canned whole, diced or crushed plum tomatoes are also good. Small cherry tomatoes, barely bigger than the fruit after which they are descriptively named, also have

a pronounced flavor that makes them ideal candidates for pasta dishes during their peak summer season. Store fresh tomatoes of any kind in a cool, dark place; refrigeration causes them to break down quickly. Use within a few days of purchase.

TO PEEL AND SEED A FRESH TOMATO

1. Bring a saucepan of water to a boil. Using a small, sharp knife, cut out the core of the tomato. Cut a shallow X in the opposite end.

2. Submerge the tomato for about 10 seconds in the boiling water, then remove and dip in a bowl of cold water.

3. Starting at the X, peel the skin, using your fingertips and, if necessary, the knife blade. Cut the tomatoes in half crosswise.

4. To seed, hold the tomato upside down and squeeze it gently to force out the seed sacs.

BASIC RECIPES

Use these basic recipes as listed in the recipes in this volume or to create your own toppings for commercial ravioli, tortellini or other filled pasta.

BROWN BUTTER

Also called beurre noisette, *brown butter is made by cooking Clarified Butter until it is amber, resulting in a nutty flavor.*

½ cup (4 oz/125 g) unsalted butter

1. In a small saucepan over medium-low heat, melt the butter, skimming off and discarding the foam that forms on the top. Continue to heat the butter over medium heat until it begins to brown.
2. Using a spoon, transfer the butter to a small container, discarding the solids at the bottom of the pan. Use immediately or store in a tightly covered container in the refrigerator for up to 1 week.

Makes 6 tablespoons (¹/₃ cup/3 fl oz/80 ml)

CLARIFIED BUTTER

Also known as drawn butter, clarified butter is butter with the milk solids removed. It can withstand higher heat for cooking.

½ cup (4 oz/125 g) unsalted butter

1. In a small saucepan over medium-low heat, melt the butter, skimming off and discarding the foam that forms on the top.

2. Using a spoon, transfer the butter to a small container, leaving behind and discarding the solids at the bottom of the pan. Use immediately or store in a tightly covered container in the refrigerator for up to 1 week.

Makes 6 tablespoons (¹/₃ cup/3 fl oz/80 ml)

GINGER BUTTER

Add herbs and spices to unsalted butter and use it on pasta, breads and rolls.

½ cup (4 oz/125 g) unsalted butter at room temperature
1 tablespoon grated fresh ginger with its juice
2 teaspoons grated lemon zest
½ teaspoon salt
½ teaspoon sugar
½ teaspoon freshly ground pepper

1. In the work bowl of a food processor with the metal blade or a blender, combine the butter, ginger, lemon zest, salt, sugar and pepper.
2. Pulse several times until the mixture is smooth. If necessary, using a rubber spatula, scrape the sides of the work bowl and pulse again.
3. Transfer the mixture to a small container or ice cube tray or place the mixture on waxed paper and roll into a cylinder. Cover and refrigerate for 2–24 hours or freeze for up to 1 month.

Makes ½ cup (4 oz/125 g)

BÉCHAMEL SAUCE

This traditional white sauce can be used as a pasta topping or as a base for other sauces. It can be made less rich by using half & half (half cream) in place of the heavy (double) cream. This recipe can be easily cut in half.

¼ cup (2 oz/60 g) unsalted butter

2 shallots, peeled and minced

¼ cup (1½ oz/45 g) all-purpose (plain) flour

2 cups (16 fl oz/500 ml) milk

1 cup (8 fl oz/250 ml) heavy (double) cream

 Salt

 Ground white pepper

1. In a medium saucepan over medium-low heat, melt the butter. Add the shallots and sauté until soft, about 5 minutes. Add the flour and cook, stirring frequently, for 3 minutes. Do not let it brown. Using a whisk, slowly mix in the milk and cream. Reduce the heat to medium-low and simmer, stirring frequently, until the sauce thickens, about 8 minutes. Remove from the heat and add salt and pepper to taste. Use at once or cover and refrigerate for up to 1 day.

Makes about 3 cups (24 fl oz/750 ml)

BOLOGNESE SAUCE

This classic meat sauce can be refrigerated for up to 1 week.

3 tablespoons pure olive oil

1 yellow onion, peeled and diced

1 celery stalk, finely chopped

1 small carrot, peeled and finely chopped

1 lb (500 g) lean ground (minced) beef

¾ cup (6 fl oz/180 ml) milk

¾ cup (6 fl oz/180 ml) dry white wine

3 lb (1.5 kg) plum (Roma) tomatoes, peeled, seeded and diced *(see page 124)* or 28 oz (875 g) canned tomatoes

6 oz (185 g) canned tomato sauce

 Ground nutmeg

 Salt

 Red pepper flakes

1. In a large, heavy frying pan over medium-low heat, heat the olive oil. Add the onion and sauté, stirring frequently, until it is translucent, about 8 minutes. Add the celery and carrots and sauté, stirring frequently, for 10 minutes.
2. Add the beef, breaking it up with a fork, and sauté, stirring frequently, until the beef just loses its color.
3. Stir in the milk and simmer until it has evaporated, about 8 minutes. Add the wine and simmer until it has evaporated, about 8 minutes longer.
4. Add the tomatoes, tomato sauce and nutmeg, salt and red pepper flakes to taste. Increase the heat to medium, bring the sauce to a simmer then reduce the heat to very low. Simmer for at least 2½ hours or up to 4 hours.

Makes about 4 cups (32 fl oz/1 l)

CHICKEN STOCK

Homemade stock adds wonderful flavor to many pasta recipes. If you must substitute, use lowfat, low-sodium canned or frozen broth. If you use leftover parts from a cooked bird, do not roast it with the vegetables.

1 yellow onion, peeled and cut into quarters

1 carrot, peeled and cut into large pieces

1 celery stalk, cut into large pieces

1 leek, white part and 2 inches (5 cm) green part, cut into large pieces

2 tablespoons pure olive oil

5 lb (2.5 kg) chicken parts (backs, necks, meaty carcasses and wings)

6 qt (6 l) water

1. Preheat an oven to 325°F (165°C).
2. In a large bowl, toss the onion, carrot, celery and leek with the olive oil. Transfer the vegetables to a large roasting pan. Add the chicken parts. Roast until the vegetables are tender and just beginning to color, about 30 minutes.
3. In a large pot over high heat, combine the vegetables, chicken, any pan drippings and the water and bring to a boil. Reduce the heat to medium-low and simmer, partially covered, until the liquid is reduced by half, about 3½ hours. Cool to room temperature.
4. Using a strainer, strain the stock into a large bowl. Refrigerate until the fat on the surface solidifies. Before using, remove and discard the surface fat. Store in a tightly covered container in the refrigerator for 5 days or freezer for 3 months.

Makes about 3 qt (3 l)

PRESERVED LEMONS

Preserved lemons have an enticing flavor that lends brightness to a variety of dishes. They are Middle Eastern in origin but warrant space in any pantry. Although they must age for at least 7 days, preparation time is minimal. In addition to recipes that call for them, use them as a condiment with grilled, roasted or stewed meats or poultry.

4 lemons

¼ cup (2 oz/60 g) kosher salt

1 tablespoon sugar

½ cup (4 fl oz/125 ml) fresh lemon juice

1. Wash and thoroughly dry the lemons. Using a sharp knife, cut each lemon crosswise into 6 slices. Remove and discard the seeds. In a small bowl, combine the lemons, salt and sugar.
2. Pack the lemons into an impeccably clean dry pint jar. Pour in the lemon juice. Cover the jar with plastic wrap and place its lid on tightly.
3. Set the jar of lemons in a cool dark place for at least 7 days. Every other day, turn it upside down so that all of the lemon slices are evenly bathed in the juice. Preserved lemons will keep in the refrigerator for up to 2 months.

Makes 1 pt (2 cups/12 oz/370 g)

CARAMELIZED ONIONS

Slow cooking turns these onions sweet. Slice each piece close in size for even cooking. This recipe can easily be reduced.

½ cup (4 fl oz/125 ml) Clarified Butter
  (recipe on page 123) or pure olive oil
5 lb (2.5 kg) yellow onions, peeled, halved
  and very thinly sliced

1. In a large, heavy frying pan over medium heat, heat the butter or olive oil. Add the onions, cover the pan and cook, stirring occasionally, until the onions are completely limp, 10–15 minutes. Remove the lid, reduce the heat to medium-low and cook, stirring frequently, until the onions are golden brown and sweet, 35–45 minutes. Do not let them burn. Remove from the heat, cool, cover and refrigerate for up to 10 days or freeze for up to 2 months.

Makes 4 cups (14 oz/435 g)

PANCETTA AND LEEK SAUCE

Be sure to wash leeks thoroughly before using in any recipe.

2 tablespoons extra-virgin olive oil
1 lb (500 g) leeks, white parts and 2 inches
  (5 cm) green parts, cut into thin rounds
4 oz (125 g) pancetta, finely chopped
1 cup (8 fl oz/250 ml) Chicken Stock
  (recipe on page 125)
2 tablespoons fresh lemon juice
  Salt and freshly ground pepper

1. Preheat an oven to 375°F (190°C). In an ovenproof frying pan, combine the olive oil, leeks and pancetta. Bake until the leeks are fragrant and tender, about 30 minutes. Place the frying pan on the stove top over medium heat. Add the Chicken Stock and the lemon juice, reduce the heat to low and simmer for 15 minutes. Add salt and pepper to taste. Reheat before serving.

Makes about 1½ cups (12 fl oz/375 ml)

PEPPER SAUCE

This smooth-textured, robust-tasting sauce can be used to top pasta or vegetables.

1 tablespoon olive oil
1 large shallot, peeled and minced
2 garlic cloves, peeled and minced
⅓ cup (3 fl oz/80 ml) dry white wine
1½ cups (12 fl oz/375 ml) Chicken Stock
  (recipe on page 125)
2 large red bell peppers (capsicums),
  roasted, peeled, seeded, deribbed and
  diced *(see page 121)*
1 tablespoon minced fresh mint leaves
  Salt and freshly ground pepper

1. In a medium saucepan over medium heat, heat the olive oil. Add the shallot and sauté until tender, 5 minutes. Add the garlic and sauté for 2 minutes. Add the wine, increase the heat to medium and simmer until almost completely evaporated, about 10 minutes. Add the Chicken Stock and simmer until it is reduced to 1 cup (8 fl oz/250 ml), about 10 minutes. Stir in the peppers and simmer for 8 minutes. Add the mint and

salt and pepper to taste. Using a food mill or a blender, purée the sauce. Set aside until ready to use.

Makes about 1 1/2 cups (12 fl oz/375 ml)

PESTO SAUCE

When basil is abundant in the garden, farmers' market or store, consider doubling or tripling this recipe and putting the extra sauce in glass canning jars. The sauce will keep in the freezer for months, bringing a taste of summer to your winter table.

2   cups (2 oz/60 g) packed fresh basil leaves
6   garlic cloves, peeled
1/2 teaspoon salt
1/4 cup (1 oz/30 g) pine nuts
1/2 cup (4 fl oz/125 ml) extra-virgin olive oil
3   tablespoons unsalted butter, softened
1/3 cup (1 1/2 oz/45 g) freshly grated Parmesan cheese

1. In the work bowl of a food processor with the metal blade or a blender, combine the basil and garlic. Pulse until the basil is very finely chopped. Add the salt and pine nuts and pulse several times. With the motor running, slowly pour in the olive oil in a steady stream.
2. Transfer the mixture to a small bowl. Using a spatula, fold in the butter and, when incorporated smoothly, fold in the Parmesan cheese.

Makes 1 cup (8 fl oz/250 ml)

SUMMER TOMATO SAUCE

Make this sauce with the best-quality tomatoes you can find. When fresh tomatoes are not available, substitute 48 oz (1.5 kg) of canned whole tomatoes.

6   tablespoons (3 oz/90 g) unsalted butter
1   yellow onion, peeled and cut into quarters
4   garlic cloves, peeled
3   lb (1.5 kg) tomatoes, halved
     Salt and freshly ground pepper

1. In a large, heavy frying pan over medium heat, melt 3 tablespoons of the butter. Add the onion, garlic and tomatoes, reduce the heat to low, cover the pan and simmer for 20 minutes. Remove the pan from the heat. Remove and discard the onion and garlic. Using a food mill or a blender, purée the tomatoes.
2. Clean the frying pan and return the tomato purée to the pan. Place over medium heat and simmer for 10 minutes. Add the remaining butter, 1 tablespoon at a time, stirring until the butter is incorporated. Add salt and pepper to taste.

Makes 1 3/4 cups (14 fl oz/430 ml)

INDEX

Agnolotti Floating in
    Mushroom Broth, 99
Angel Hair Pasta Flan, 67
Apricot and Wine Sauce, 38

Béchamel Sauce, 124
Beet Pasta, 10
Beet Fazzoletti with Orange
    Vinaigrette, 103
Black Pepper Pasta, 10
Bolognese Lasagne, 48
Bolognese Sauce, 124
Bread crumbs, 116
Brown Butter, 123

Cannelloni Primavera with
    Pepper Sauce, 91
Caponata Filled Shells with
    Béchamel Sauce, 108
Caramelized Onion and
    Pancetta Lasagne, 55
Caramelized Onions, 126
Cheese Crespelle with
    Sweet Tomato Sauce, 95
Chicken Ravioli with
    Marsala Cream Sauce,
    41
Chicken Stock, 125
Clarified Butter, 123
Crab Ravioli with Hot
    Lemon Butter Sauce, 34
Crespelle, making, 13
Curried-Potato and Pea
    Ravioli with Yogurt
    Sauce, 30

Eggs, separating, 118

Farfalline with Olives and
    Sun-Dried Tomatoes, 63
Fresh Lasagne with Basil
    and Béchamel Sauce, 52
Frittata of Capellini,
    Onions and Pancetta, 75
Fruits, zesting, 118

Garlic, preparing, 119
Ginger, preparing, 119
Ginger Butter, 123
Goat Cheese Sauce, 88
Gorgonzola Cream Sauce,
    115

Hot Lemon Butter, 34

Italian Meatballs, 76

Lamb Filled Shells with
    Tomato and Lemon
    Sauce, 112
Lasagne Pinwheels with
    Pancetta and Leek
    Sauce, 100
Leeks, cleaning, 120
Lemon Pasta, 10
Lemon Cream Sauce, 22
Lemon Ravioli with
    Pumpkin Filling, 33
Lemony Linguine and
    Crab in Parchment, 68

Macaroni and Cheese with
    Bacon, 64
Manicotti with Greens and
    Spicy Tomato Sauce, 87
Manicotti with Mushrooms
    and Goat Cheese
    Sauce, 88

Nutritional analysis, 9
Nuts, toasting, 120

One-Pound Egg Pasta, 10
Orange Vinaigrette, 103
Orzo in Tomato Broth
    with a Cheese Crust, 59
Orzo with Winter Squash
    and Leeks, 60

Pancetta and Leek Sauce,
    126

Pappardelle with Summer
    Tomato Sauce, 80
Pasta
    cooking, 18–19
    dried, 16
    ingredients, 10
    making fresh, 10–15
Pasta Carbonara Soufflé,
    72
Pennette and Bean Soup
    with a Cheese Crust,
    56
Pepper Sauce, 126
Peppers, preparing, 121
Pesto Sauce, 127
Pork and Dried Apricot
    Ravioli with Apricot
    and Wine Sauce, 38
Potato and Garlic Ravioli
    with Brown Butter, 25
Pound-and-a-Half Egg
    Pasta, 11
Preserved Lemons, 125

Radiatori Bolognese with
    Italian Meatballs, 76
Ravioli, making, 14–15
Ricotta Filled Shells with
    Bolognese Sauce, 107

Saffron Pasta, 10
Sage Cream Sauce, 37
Sage-Scented Semolina
    Gnocchi with
        Mozzarella, 79
Seafood Crespelle with
    Cherry Tomatoes, 92
Shallot Vinaigrette, 104
Shrimp, peeling and
    deveining, 122
Smoked Salmon Ravioli
    with Lemon Cream
    Sauce, 22
Spaghettini and Scallops
    in Parchment, 71

Spicy Tomato Sauce, 87
Spinach Pasta, 10
Spinach Pasta Rolls with
    Summer Tomato
    Sauce, 111
Spinach Ravioli with
    Summer Tomato
    Sauce, 45
Spinach Tortellini with
    Gorgonzola Cream
    Sauce, 115
Squash, 60
Stacked Pasta Rounds
    with Lamb and
    Eggplant, 84
Summer Tomato Sauce, 127
Sweet Potato Crespelle
    with Walnut Sauce, 96
Sweet Tomato Sauce, 95
Swiss Chard Fazzoletti
    with Shallot
        Vinaigrette, 104

Three-Cheese Ravioli with
    Greens and Walnuts, 26
Tomato, Anchovy and
    Artichoke Heart
        Lasagne, 51
Tomato and Lemon Sauce,
    112
Tomato Pasta, 10
Tomatoes, peeling and
    seeding, 122
Turkey and Sage Ravioli
    with Sage Cream
    Sauce, 37
Two-Toned Ravioli with
    Pesto Sauce, 29

Walnut Butter Sauce, 42
Walnut Sauce, 96
Wild Rice Ravioli
    with Walnut Butter
    Sauce, 42